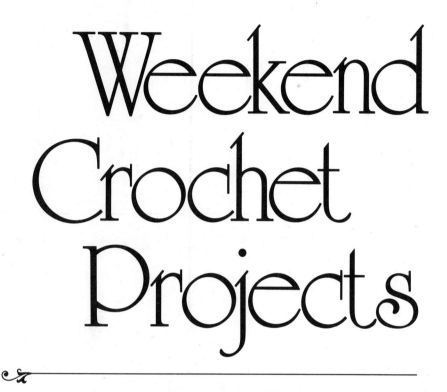

Weekend Crochet Projects

Margaret Hubert

VAN NOSTRAND REINHOLD COMPANY
New York Cincinnati Toronto London Melbourne

For Mom

Photography by Christopher Hubert and Robert M. Hubert

Copyright © 1981 by Litton Educational Publishing, Inc.
Library of Congress Catalog Card Number 80-22184
ISBN 0-442-23850-9

Printed in the United States of America

Book design by Charlotte Staub

Published in 1981 by Van Nostrand Reinhold Company
A division of Litton Educational Publishing, Inc.
135 West 50th Street, New York, N.Y. 10020

Van Nostrand Reinhold Limited
1410 Birchmount Road, Scarborough, Ontario M1P 2E7, Canada

Van Nostrand Reinhold Australia Pty, Ltd.
17 Queen Street, Mitcham, Victoria 3132, Australia

Van Nostrand Reinhold Company Limited
Molly Millars Lane, Wokingham, Berkshire, England

16 15 14 13 12 11 10 9 8 7 6 5 4 3 2 1

Library of Congress Cataloging in Publication Data

Hubert, Margaret.
  Weekend crochet projects.

  Includes index.
  1. Crocheting. I. Title.
TT820.H84   746.43′4   80-22184
ISBN 0-442-23850-9

contents

acknowledgments

While finishing up the last few pages of this book, I began to wonder how I might best express my gratitude to all the people who have helped me in its preparation. I started out with all kinds of flowery comments, kudos, bouquets, etc. and ended by tearing up many pages. Finally, I decided that the best way is to just say many thanks to all.

I want to especially thank Susan Rosenthal Gies, my editor, who is the calmest person I know and a joy to work with; Nancy N. Green, editor-in-chief of Van Nostrand Reinhold, who is ever encouraging; my husband and son, who did all the photography; my mother, Carmela Mancuso; my friends, Mary Bauer, Dora Filippi (whose lovely sweater is shown on the book jacket), and Marguerite Parkin, who helped me crochet many of the garments; John Lawler for his many hours of time, advice, and guidance; the yarn companies who donated yarn; the models without whom there would not have been a book; and Joseph, Allen, and Andrew, the staff of Bronxville Camera, for their help and patience.

Last, but not least, special thanks must go to Sharon E. Hubert for her original designs: Granny Shawl, Child's Hat and Scarf, Baby's Sacque and Hat, Baby's Raglan Pullover, and Toddler's Hooded Sweatshirt.

A final word of thanks to each and every one of the models:

Kim Bason	Laura Ghirardi	Pam Mancuso
Grace Brennan	Christopher Hubert	Dana A. Mills
Joseph J. Campanaro	Robert Hubert	Darby A. Mills
Virely M. Davis	Valerie Hubert	Melissa Montagino
Philip J. Federico	Dawn Lavender	Lorraine Parkin
Stacy Federico	Celeste Lawler	Martin Parkin
Christina Filippi	Barbara Mancuso	Melissa Savino
Linda Filippi	Cheri Mancuso	Angela Sheehy
Erica Fredrickson	Louis G. Mancuso	Rachel Stevens

manufacturers of large crochet hooks

C.J. Bates and Sons, Inc.
Susan Bates
Chester, Conn. 06412;

Mokena, Ill. 60477; and
Redwood City, Calif. 94063

Boye
A Newell Company
Freeport, Ill. 61032

Emile Bernat and Sons, Inc.
Aero Knitting Needles and
  Crochet Hooks
Uxbridge, Mass. 01569

4

Recently there has been a revival of interest in handcrafts, with a particularly strong resurgence in crochet. This interest seems to come from the desire within us all to create something on our own. Yet another reason for this renewed popularity in crochet is that many of the country's top fashion designers have added hand knits and crochets to their collections. The fashion conscious woman who can knit or crochet can make herself a very special wardrobe. What's more, she can surprise her friends and relatives with lovely handmade gifts, a great source of satisfaction for both giver and receiver.

Many people believe that hand work such as this must be very time-consuming and that they couldn't possibly devote the many hours that must be necessary to achieve these beautiful results. Here is a pleasant surprise!

Weekend Crochet Projects is just what the title indicates. It is a collection of very wearable, very beautiful, items that can literally be made in one weekend. Some can even be made in an evening. Whether you are a busy mother and homemaker, or a career woman, you will be able to complete dozens of these lovely projects without having to disrupt your busy schedule.

Crochet designs can be very simple or very complex. For the purposes of this book, I have used very simple designs and techniques; they are the most fun to do and they go quickly. Because the stitches are so simple, and, because you will be using bulky yarns and very large hooks, the projects simply fly. What's more, the simple stitches take on a whole new dimension when worked with bulky yarn and large hooks. Single crochet, the simplest of all crochet stitches, for example, looks deeply textured and intricate when done with an N hook and bulky yarn.

A word about hooks: There are a variety of hooks available on the market, but not all crochet hook manufacturers produce all sizes, and there is a lack of uniformity among these larger hooks. In some instances, where there is only one manufacturer who makes a particular size, I have specified the company name. If I have specified wood, or aluminum, or plastic, this means that at this time the size is only available in that material. If it should happen that these large hooks are not available in your area, most companies will mail-order to you or will supply you with sources for mail-ordering. (See page 4 for names and addresses of hook manufacturers.)

As anyone who has ever crocheted will tell you, "time flies when you're having fun." I know you will have fun this weekend, or any time during the week, for that matter, as you sit back and create your first Weekend Crochet Project.

introduction

helpful hints for weekend crocheters

In working with very bulky yarns (or two strands of yarn held together) and with very large hooks, it is necessary to bend the rules occasionally. The following tips will help you out:

- When sewing seams, hold pieces to be sewn together on a flat surface and weave the seams with a close back-and-forth stitch. This will make a very flat seam.

- As far as blocking is concerned, never block heavily textured crochet. It will flatten your stitches and make your work appear lifeless.

- When working with two or more strands of yarn, it is helpful to put each yarn in a separate bag. Keeping them separate as you work will prevent tangles, will allow you to work at a faster pace, and will eliminate frazzled nerves also.

- These garments are designed to be made quickly, with a minimum of finishing. Do not be afraid to experiment a little, changing patterns or colors to create your own look.

- It is crucial that whatever yarn you choose meets the same gauge as specified in the directions or the garment will not fit properly. No matter how beautiful, if the fit is not right, your efforts will be wasted.

- To determine correct size for a crocheted garment, take body measurements at fullest part of chest, hips, and natural waistline. Allowances have been made for ease and proper fit. Use the size that is nearest to the chest measurement. Other adjustments may be made in the blocking or while you are working the pattern. Refer to the following chart.

Infants' and Toddlers' Sizes

	6 mos	1	2	3	4
Chest:	19	20	21	22	23
Waist:	20	19½	20	20½	21
Hips:	20	21	22	23	24
Height:	22	25	29	31	33

Children's Sizes

	4	6	8	10	12	14
Chest:	23	24	26	28	30	32
Waist:	21	22	23½	24½	25½	26½
Hips	24	26	28	30	32	34

Young Men's or Women's Sizes

	8	10	12	14	16
Chest:	28	29	31	33	34
Waist:	23	24	25	26	29
Hips:	31	32	34	36	38

Women's Sizes

	8	10	12	14	16	18
Chest:	31½	32½	34	36	38	40
Waist:	23	24	25½	27	29	31
Hips:	33½	34½	36	38	40	42

Men's Sizes

	34	36	38	40	42	44	46
Chest:	34	36	38	40	42	44	46
Waist:	30	32	34	36	38	40	42

The terms that follow are important parts of a crocheter's vocabulary. The list will serve as a crash course for the novice and as a refresher course for the more experienced crocheter.

the language
of crochet

Brackets [ ]:   Used to help you keep track of how many of a particular type of stitch has been made.

Cardigan: A type of garment that opens down the front and uses a zipper or buttons for closing.

Cap sleeve: A type of sleeve that just covers a small portion of the upper arm.

Cowl neck: A loose, high collar, that is folded in half, draping into a soft ring around the neck.

Decrease: Unless otherwise specified, this means to draw up a loop in each of two stitches, then work it off as one stitch.

Double crochet: Yarn over hook once, pick up a loop in the next stitch, yarn over hook, and draw through two loops, yarn over hook, and draw through remaining two loops.

Fringe: To make a fringe, wrap yarn around a piece of cardboard, about 1 inch longer than desired length of finished fringe. Using a crochet hook, pull folded piece of yarn through one end of work, about 1 inch, then pull ends through the loop and knot. Cut opposite end of wrapped yarn. Strands of yarn may be doubled or tripled for thicker fringes.

Half double crochet: Yarn over hook, pull up a loop in next stitch, yarn over hook, and pull through all three loops.

Increase: Unless otherwise specified, this means to make two stitches in one stitch.

Joining yarn: This is best done at the outside edges of the garment by tying a knot, leaving long ends that can later be woven into the seam.

Kimono sleeve: A long, loose sleeve that is straight and just as wide at the bottom as it is at upper arm.

One-piece crocheting: This can be a raglan sleeve made from the top down or a T top. The term refers to garments that include sleeve and body in one, so that there is very little or no seaming to be done.

Parentheses ( ):   Used to enclose directions for larger sizes and also to indicate that the instructions enclosed within are to be repeated for a specific number of times.

Pick up stitches: Refers to working stitches that are not in continuation of the piece being worked. For example, you would pick up stitches along a neckline, or side of a garment section.

Picot edge: Work a picot edging along a finished edge as follows: Chain 3, make 1 single crochet in the base of the chain 3, skip 1 stitch, and make a single crochet in the next stitch. Repeat all across edge.

Pom-pom: To make a pom-pom, wind yarn about 150 times around a 2-inch piece of cardboard. Slip yarn off cardboard and tie securely in center. Cut each end, shake vigorously, and trim to form a round ball.

Popcorn stitch: There are many variations of a popcorn stitch. In this book I have used an easy version. Yarn over hook and pull up a long loop three times. Then yarn over hook and pull through all but last loop. Yarn over and pull through remaining two loops.

Pullover: Any garment that is made without a front opening and that must be pulled over the head.

Raglan sleeve: A loose-fitting sleeve that is worked from the armhole up to the neck on the diagonal, rather than fitting on the shoulder as would a conventional sleeve.

Shawl collar: A big, turned-back collar that wraps the back of the neck and forms a V shape in front. Can be made with pullovers or cardigans.

Single crochet: The simplest of all crochet stitches and the most versatile. Yarn over hook, pick up a loop in the next stitch, yarn over hook, and pull through both loops.

Slip stitch: Pick up a loop in next stitch, then pull same loop through the stitch on hook.

T top: A garment made with the sleeve as part of the body in the shape of a T.

Triple crochet: Yarn over hook twice, pick up a loop in the next stitch, yarn over hook, and bring through two loops, yarn over and bring through remaining two loops on hook.

Turtleneck: A high, close-fitting collar that hugs the neck snugly, usually made about 6 inches high, then folded in half.

V neck: A neckline that forms a V shape in front. It can be made on a cardigan or a pullover.

Yarn over: Wrap yarn around hook, forming another loop on hook.

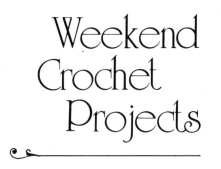

Weekend
Crochet
Projects

Woman's Short, Curly Sweater
This sweater is one of the easiest projects in the book. You can make it in a jiffy and wear it with just about any outfit in your wardrobe.

woman's short, curly sweater

Women's Sizes

Directions are for size 8. Changes for sizes 10 and 12 are in parentheses.

Materials

10 (11, 12) skeins (1.7 oz or 50 g each) Rhumba Yarn by Unger, or any curly yarn to give gauge

Hook

Size 10½ or K

Gauge

2 stitches = 1 inch (2.5 cm)

Note: Yarn is used double strand throughout.

Back

With size 10½ hook, chain 36 (38, 40).
Foundation row: Make 1 double crochet in 3rd chain from hook, make 1 double crochet in each chain across row [34 (36, 38) double crochets].
Row 1: Chain 3 to turn, skip the first stitch [chain 3 counts as the first double crochet], make 1 double crochet in each stitch across row, make 1 double crochet in top of the turning chain.

Continue to repeat Row 1 till 10 (11, 12) inches (25, 27.5, 30 cm), or desired length to underarm. Slip stitch over 3 stitches, work to within 3 stitches of other side, chain 3, and turn. Continuing in pattern as established, decrease 1 stitch each side, every row, 2 times. Work even on the remaining 24 (26, 28) stitches till armhole is 7 (7½, 8) inches (17.5, 18.8, 20 cm), end off.

Left Front

Chain 18 (19, 20). Work pattern same as Back to armhole. Shape arm sides as Back, work till armhole is 5 (5½, 6) inches (12.5, 13.8, 15 cm), ending at front edge. Shape neck as follows: slip stitch over 3 stitches, then decrease 1 stitch neck edge, every row, 1 (2, 2) time(s). Work even, if necessary, to shoulder, end off.

Right Front

Work same as Left Front, reversing all armhole and neck shaping.

Sleeves

With size 10½ hook, chain 17 (18, 19). Work pattern same as Back, increasing 1 stitch each side, every 2 inches (5 cm), 5 (5, 6) times. Work even till 16 (17, 18) inches (40, 42.5, 45 cm), or desired length to underarm. Slip stitch over 3 stitches, work to within 3 stitches of other side, then decrease 1 stitch each side, every row, 5 (6, 7) times. Work even 1 row, end off.

Finishing

Sew seams. Using size 10½ hook double strand of yarn, and with right side facing you, start at bottom right seam and work 1 row single crochet around all outside edges, making 3 single crochets in each corner to turn. Work 1 row single crochet around bottom of Sleeves. Do not block.

man's rugged turtleneck pullover

Men's Sizes
Directions are for size 36–38. Changes for sizes 40–42 and 44–46 are in parentheses.

Materials
9 (10, 11) skeins (3.5 oz or 100 g each) Germantown Knitting Worsted by Brunswick, or any knitting worsted to give gauge

Hook
Size 10 or K
Boye aluminum size N

Gauge
2 single crochets = 1 inch (2.5 cm)

Note: Yarn is used double strand throughout.

Back
With larger hook, chain 39 (41, 43).
Foundation row: Work 1 single crochet in 2nd chain from hook, 1 single crochet in each stitch across row [38 (40, 42) single crochets].
Row 1: Chain 1, turn, skip the first stitch [chain 1 counts as the first stitch], work 1 single crochet in each stitch to end of row.

Repeat Row 1 till 16 (16½, 17) inches (41, 41.3, 42.5 cm) from beginning, or desired length to underarm. Slip stitch over 3 stitches, work to within 3 stitches of other side, chain, and turn. Continuing in pattern as established, decrease 1 stitch each side, every row, 3 times. Work even till armhole is 9½ (9½, 10) inches (23.8, 23.8, 25 cm), end off.

Front
Work same as Back till armhole is 7½ (7½, 8) inches (18.8, 18.8, 20 cm). Work across 10 stitches, chain 1, and turn. Working this section only, decrease 1 stitch neck edge, every row, 3 times. Work even to shoulder, bind off. Skip the center stitches and work 10 stitches other side to correspond.

Sleeves
Chain 20 (22, 24). Work in single crochet same as Back, increasing 1 stitch each side, every 3 inches (7.5 cm), 5 (5, 6) times. Work even till 17 (17½, 18) inches (42.5, 43.8, 45 cm) from the beginning, or desired length to underarm. Slip stitch over 3 stitches, work to within 3 stitches of other side, chain, and turn. Continuing in pattern, decrease 1 stitch each side, every row, 8 (9, 10) times. Work even 2 rows, end off.

Collar
With smaller hook, chain 16. Work in single crochet from the back loop for 21 (21, 22) inches (52.5, 52.5, 55 cm), end off.

Finishing
Sew shoulders. Sew underarm seams. Sew short ends of Collar together, then, centering seam at back of neck, sew Collar in place. Do not block.

Man's Rugged Turtleneck Pullover
Men love the sporty good looks of a turtleneck sweater. Terrific for all outdoor activities,
this rugged pullover is easy to make and comfortable to wear.

Toddler's Box-Stitched Vest

The unusual box stitch gives this little vest its interesting texture. It's the perfect gift for a toddler.

Toddlers' Sizes
Directions are for size 1. Changes for sizes 2 and 3 are in parentheses.

Materials
2 (2, 2) skeins (3.5 oz or 100 g each) Red Heart 4-ply Knitting Worsted by Coats & Clark, or any knitting worsted to give gauge
5 buttons

Hook
Boye aluminum size N

Gauge
1 cluster = 1 inch (2.5 cm)
To save time, take the time to check gauge.

Note: Yarn is worked double strand throughout.
   Vest is worked in 1 piece with a seam only at shoulder.

Fronts and Lower Back
With size N hook, chain 53 (56, 59).
Foundation row: Work 1 double crochet in 3rd chain from hook, 1 double crochet in each chain thereafter [50 (53, 56) double crochets].
Row 1: Chain 1 to turn, make 1 single crochet in space between first 2 double crochets, *chain 3, skip 3 double crochets, make 1 single crochet in next space, repeat from * across row, ending with 1 single crochet between the last 2 double crochets [16 (17, 18) chain 3 loops].
Row 2: Chain 3 to turn, work 3 double crochets, chain 1 in each chain-3 loop across row, end with 1 double crochet in top of the turning chain [16 (17, 18) clusters].
   Repeat Rows 1 and 2 3 (4, 4) times more. Work across 4 clusters, chain, and turn. Working on this section only, decrease 1 stitch each side, every row, 3 times. [*To decrease:* have 1 stitch less in the chain or the cluster each time.] Then, continuing in pattern, decrease front edge only, every row, 5 times. Work even till 9 (10, 10) complete patterns have been made, end off. Join yarn 4 clusters in from other side, and complete as other side, reversing all shaping.

Back Upper Section
Join yarn in same space that Front section ends off, work Back on the center 8 (9, 10) clusters. Decrease 1 stitch each side of Back, every row, 4 (5, 6) times. Work even to shoulder, end off.

Finishing
Sew shoulder seams. Work 2 rows single crochet around armholes and front and neck edges. Sew on 5 buttons and button in the open spaces of stitches. Do not block.

toddler's box-stitched vest

baby's one-piece pullover

Infants' Sizes
Directions are for size 9 months. Changes for 18 months and 2 years are in parentheses.

Materials
2 skeins (3.5 oz or 100 g each) Red Heart 4-ply Knitting Worsted by Coats & Clark, or any knitting worsted to give gauge—1 skein each in Colors A and B

Hook
Size 8 or H

Gauge
3 stitches = 1 inch (2.5 cm)
To save time, take the trouble to check gauge.

Note: The sweater is a raglan sleeve, worked in 1 piece from the neck down.

Yoke

With size 8 hook, chain 55 (55, 59). Join with a slip stitch to form a ring.

Foundation row: Chain 3 [counts as first double crochet]. Working in double crochet from the back loop, make 1 double crochet in each of the next 18 (18, 20) stitches. Make 1 double crochet, chain 1, 1 double crochet, all in the next stitch [corner stitch made], make 1 double crochet in each of the next 8 stitches, 1 corner stitch in the next stitch, 1 double crochet in each of the next 18 (18, 20) stitches, 1 corner stitch in the next stitch, 1 double crochet in each of the next 8 stitches, 1 double crochet, chain 1 in the same stitch as the starting chain 3, join with a slip stitch to top of chain.

Row 1: Chain 3 [counts as half of the last corner stitch], working from the back loop throughout, *make 1 double crochet in each stitch to next corner, make corner stitch in the chain-1 space, repeat from * around, ending with 1 double crochet, chain 1 in the last chain-1 space, join with a slip stitch to starting chain 3.

Repeat Row 1 3 (4, 5) times more with Color A, 2 times with Color B. This ends Yoke section.

Body

Chain 2, work in double crochet to next corner stitch [Back], chain 2, skip the next section for Sleeve, continue in double crochet across next section [Front]. Join with a slip stitch to starting chain. Continuing round and round, work on Back and Front as 1 for 10 (11, 12) rows more. Work 2 rows single crochet, end off.

Sleeves

Joining yarn on the chain 2 at underarm, work around Sleeve, picking up every stitch. Join with a slip stitch to where you started. Chain 2, continuing in pattern as established, work 10 (11, 12) rows more. Work 1 row single crochet, decreasing every 5th stitch. Work 2 more rows single crochet, end off.

Finishing

Work 3 rows single crochet around neck, being careful not to pull in too tightly, end off. Do not block.

Baby's One-Piece Pullover
*This raglan pullover, made from the top down, is very easy to do because it is made
in one piece. Sweaters made in this way require very little sewing when finished.*

Young Woman's Cross-Stitched Pullover
This versatile pullover with a drawstring bottom and contrasting color trim is a terrific addition to any wardrobe. The interesting cross-stitch is made very easily with double crochet stitches.

Young Women's Sizes

Directions are for size 10. Changes for sizes 12 and 14 are in parentheses.

Materials

5 (5, 6) skeins (3.5 oz or 100 g each) Germantown Knitting Worsted by Brunswick, or any knitting worsted to give gauge—4 (4, 5) skeins in Color A, 1 in Color B

Hook   **Gauge**

Size 8 or H   2 cross-stitches = 1 inch (2.5 cm)

Pattern

Row 1 in single crochet   Row 2 in cross-stitch

Back

With size 8 hook, chain 65 (69, 73).

Foundation row: Work 1 single crochet in 2nd chain from hook, 1 single crochet in each chain across row [64 (68, 72) single crochets].

Row 1: Chain 3 to turn [chain 3 counts as a double crochet], skip 2 stitches, make 1 double crochet in the next stitch, make 1 double crochet in the 2nd stitch skipped, *skip 1 stitch, make 1 double crochet in the next stitch, make 1 double crochet in the skipped stitch [cross-stitch made], repeat from * across row, end the row 1 double crochet in the last stitch. [You will have 62 (66, 70) cross-stitches and 1 double crochet at each end of row.]

Row 2: Chain 1 to turn, skip the first stitch [chain 1 counts as the first single crochet], make 1 single crochet in each stitch across row.

   Repeat Rows 1 and 2 till piece measures 16 (16½, 17) inches (41, 41.3, 42.5 cm) from beginning, end off.

Front

Work same as Back till piece measures 13 (13½, 14) inches (33.5, 34.8, 35 cm), then shape neck as follows: work across 7 (8, 9) cross-stitches, chain, and turn. Work on this section only till same length as Back, end off. Skip the center 16 cross-stitches, join yarn, and work other shoulder to correspond.

Sleeves

Chain and work foundation row and pattern same as Back for 12 (13, 14) inches (31, 33.5, 35 cm), end off.

Finishing

Sew shoulders. Sew sides leaving 6 (6½, 7) inches (15, 16.3, 17.5 cm) open for armhole. Fold Sleeve in half longways and sew seam. Using Color B, work 1 row single crochet around neckline, making 1 stitch in each space between cross-stitches. Work 1 row single crochet around top and bottom of Sleeves and around armholes. Sew Sleeves in place. Work 1 row double crochet around bottom. Using yarn double strand, chain 100 (110, 115) stitches for drawstring. Weave drawstring through the double crochet stitches at bottom. Do not block.

young woman's cross-stitched pullover

19

young woman's pullover vest

Directions are for size 10. Changes for sizes 12 and 14 are in parentheses.

Materials
2 (3, 3) skeins (3.5 oz or 100 g each) Germantown Knitting Worsted by Brunswick
6 (6, 7) skeins (1.7 oz or 50 g each) Multi Glow Yarn by Stanley Berocco, or any yarn to give gauge

Hook
Boye aluminum size N

Gauge
1½ stitches = 1 inch (2.5 cm)

Note: Yarn is used double strand throughout.

Vest is worked from the side over, joined in the center. Yarn must always be cut at the end of each row and worked from the right side.

Left Front and Back
With N hook and knitting worsted, chain 63 (65, 67).
Foundation row: Make 1 double crochet in 3rd chain from hook,1 double crochet in each stitch to end of row [60 (62, 64) double crochets]. Break knitting worsted.
Row 1: With nubby yarn, join at the beginning of the row, chain 3, work 1 double crochet in each *space* across row, end the row with 1 double crochet in the top of the last stitch, break nubby yarn.
Row 2: With knitting worsted, join at the beginning of the row, chain 3, work 1 double crochet in each *space* across row, end the row with 1 double crochet in the top of the last stitch, break knitting worsted.

Repeat Rows 1 and 2 twice more. Make side pieces as follows: starting at bottom, right side facing you, join knitting worsted in the first stitch, and work double crochet over 20 spaces, break yarn. Skip 20 (22, 24) spaces, join yarn, chain 3, and work double crochet in last 20 spaces. Make center pieces as follows: join yarn on opposite side, work double crochet in 25 spaces, break yarn, skip 15 (17, 19) spaces, and work double crochet in the last 20 spaces.

Right Front and Back
Work same as Left Front and Back, reversing side pickups.

Finishing
Sew Back seam, matching the 25 picked-up stitches to each other. Sew Front, matching the 20 picked-up stitches. Sew Sides, matching the 20 picked-up stitches on the sides. Work 2 rows of single crochet all around bottom edge, work 1 row single crochet around neck edge. Using knitting worsted, triple strand, chain 90 for Tie. Weave tie in and out spaces at waistline. Do not block.

Young Woman's Pullover Vest
*In order to achieve the vertical striping, this vest must be made from the side over.
The combination of smooth yarn with a textured yarn also creates an interesting
effect.*

mother and daughter car coats

Every little girl would love to have a car coat just like Mom's. Make one for yourself and your daughter or surprise some friends.

mother's coat

Women's Sizes
Directions are for small size. Changes for medium and large sizes are in parentheses.

Materials
6 (6, 7) skeins (3.5 oz or 100 g each) Red Heart 4-ply Yarn by Coats & Clark, or any knitting worsted to give gauge
6 buttons

Hook
Size 10½ or K

Gauge
1 cluster of 1 single crochet, 1 half double crochet, 1 single crochet = 1 inch (2.5 cm)

Note: Jacket body is worked in 1 piece from the bottom up.

22

Back and Fronts

With size 10½ hook, chain 120 (124, 128).

Foundation row: Starting in 3rd chain from hook, *make 1 single-crochet, 1 half double crochet, 1 single crochet all in the same stitch [1 shell made], skip 2 stitches, repeat from * across row, ending 1 double crochet in the last stitch [39 (40, 42) shells].

Row 1: Chain 2 to turn, *skip 2 stitches, make 1 single crochet, 1 half double crochet, 1 single crochet all in the next stitch, repeat from * across row, end 1 double crochet in the last stitch.

Continue to repeat Row 1 till 14 (15, 16) inches (35, 37.5, 40 cm) from beginning. Next row, work across 9 (9, 10) shell patterns [this is Left Front], then make 1 double crochet in the space before the next shell, chain 2, and turn. Working this 1 section only, keep front edges even, decreasing 1 stitch at arm side, every row, 3 (3, 4) times always ending the row with 1 double crochet. [*To decrease:* eliminate 1 stitch of shell each row at arm side till you have 8 (8, 9) shells left.] Work even till armhole is 5 (5½, 6) inches (12.5, 13.8, 15 cm), ending at front edge. Slip stitch over 3 shell patterns, chain 3, and work remaining stitches to end of row. Continuing in pattern, decrease 1 stitch neck edge, every row, 6 times [3 (3;4) shell patterns left.] Work even, if necessary, till armhole is 7½ (8, 8½) inches (18.8, 20, 21.3 cm), end off. Join yarn 9 (9, 10) shell patterns in from other side. Work Right Front to correspond to Left Front. For Back, skip 1 stitch at each underarm and work the 19 (20, 20) center shells as follows: decrease 1 stitch each side, every row, 3 times [17 (18, 18) shells left]. Work on the remaining shells till same as Front to shoulder, end off.

Sleeves

Chain 33 (35, 37), work same as Back, increasing 1 stitch each side, every 3rd row 3 times. [*To increase:* keep addedstitches in half double crochets. When 3 stitches are added then form a new shell pattern.] Continue in this manner, forming new patterns until there are 13 (14, 15) shells on Sleeve. Work even till Sleeve is 16 (16½, 17) inches (40, 41.3, 42.5 cm). Slip stitch over 3 stitches, work to within 3 stitches of other side, chain 2, and turn. Decrease 1 stitch each side every row till cap of Sleeve has 5 (5, 6) shells, end off. [*To decrease:* make each end shell 1 stitch less every row till that shell is totally eliminated.]

Pockets and Belt *(See photograph.)*

Chain 23 (23, 25). Work shell pattern same as Back for 5 (5, 5½) inches (12.5, 12.5, 13.8 cm), do not break yarn, chain 33 (35, 37), work pattern of the chain same as foundation row, then continue across top of Pocket. Work pattern for 1 inch (2.5 cm) more, end off.

Collar

Chain 60 (62, 62). Work patterns same as Back for 4 inches (10 cm), end off.

Side view of car coat.

Finishing

Sew shoulder seams, sew Sleeve seam, set in sleeves. Work 1 row of single crochet all around Pockets and Belt. Join with a slip stitch to first stitch, do not break yarn, do not turn. Work 1 row single crochet backwards all around Pockets and Belt, end off. Sew Pockets in place. Work same edging around 3 sides of Collar. Sew Collar in place, centering Back and having edges of Collar 2½ inches (6 cm) in from edge of sweater. Starting at bottom right side, work 1 row single crochet along front edge to top, make 3 single crochets in corner to turn, continue single crochet to edge of Collar. Join with a slipstitch, turn. Work another row of single crochet along front edge, making 4 buttonholes, starting about 6 inches (15 cm) from top, chain 1, and turn. [*To make buttonholes:* chain 2, skip 2 stitches.] Make another row of single crochet, do not turn. Work 1 row backward single crochet, end off. Starting at edge of Collar on Left Front, work border to correspond. Do not block. Sew buttons in place, tacking Belt down with buttons in back.

daughter's coat

Toddlers' Sizes

Directions are for size 2. Changes for sizes 3 and 4 are in parentheses.

Materials

3 (3, 4) skeins (3.5 oz or 100 g each) Red Heart 4-ply Yarn byCoats & Clark, or any knitting worsted to give gauge
6 buttons — 4 for Front, 2 for Belt

Hook

Size 10½ or K

Gauge

1 cluster of 1 single crochet, 1 half double crochet, 1 single crochet = 1 inch (2.5 cm)
To save time, take the time to check gauge.

Note: Jacket body is worked in 1 piece from the bottom up.

Back and Fronts

With size 10½ hook, chain 87 (93, 99).
Foundation row: Starting in 3rd chain from hook, *make 1 single crochet, 1 half double crochet, 1 single crochet all in the same stitch [1 shell made], skip 2 stitches, repeat from * across row, ending 1 double crochet in the last stitch [28 (30, 32) shells.]
Row 1: Chain 2 to turn, *skip 2 stitches, make 1 single crochet, 1 half double crochet, 1 single crochet all in the next stitch, repeat from * across row, end 1 double crochet in the last stitch.

Continue to repeat Row 1 till 8 (9, 10) inches (20, 22.5, 25 cm), or desired length to underarm. Next row, work across 6 (7, 7) shell

24

patterns [this is Left Front], then make 1 double crochet in the space before the next shell, chain 2, and turn. Working this 1 section only, keep front edges even and decrease 1 stitch at arm side, every row, 2 (2, 2) times, always ending the row with 1 double crochet. [*To decrease*: eliminate 1 stitch of shell each row at arm side till you have 5 (5, 6) shells.] Work even till armhole is 4 (4½, 5) inches (10, 11.3, 12.5 cm), ending at front edge. Slip stitch over 2 shell patterns, chain 3, and work remaining stitches to end of row. Continuing in pattern, decrease 1 stitch neck edge, every row, 3 times [2 (2, 3) patterns left]. Work even, if necessary, till armhole is 5½ (6, 6½) inches (13.8, 15, 16.3 cm), end off. Join yarn 6 (7, 7) shell patterns in from other side. Work Right Front to correspond to Left Front. For Back, skip 1 (1, 2) shell(s) at each underarm and work the center shells as follows: decrease 1 stitch each side, every row, 2 times. Work even on remaining stitches till same as Front to shoulder, end off.

Sleeves
Chain 20 (22, 24), work same as Back, increasing 1 stitch each side, every 3rd row, 3 (4, 5) times. Work even till Sleeve is 9 (9½, 10) inches (22.5, 23.8, 25 cm). Slip stitch over 1 pattern, work to within 1 pattern of other side, chain, and turn, decrease 1 stitch each side, every row, till 4 patterns remain, work 1 row even, end off.

Pockets and Belt *(See photograph.)*
Chain 13 (14, 14), work shell pattern same as Back for 4 inches (10 cm). At the end of last row, chain 23. Work pattern on the added stitches and across Pocket for 1 inch (2.5 cm) more, end off. Work same for another Pocket; reverse belt, end off.

Collar
Chain 40 (41, 42). Work pattern same as Back for 2½ (3, 3) inches (6, 7.5, 7.5 cm), end off.

Finishing
Sew shoulder seams, sew Sleeve seams, set in Sleeves. Work 1 row of single crochet all around Pockets and Belt. Join with a slip stitch to first stitch, do not break yarn, do not turn. Work 1 row single crochet backwards all around Pockets and Belt, end off. Sew pockets in place. Work same edging around 3 sides of Collar. Sew Collar in place, centering Back and having edges of Collar 1½ inches (3.8 cm) in from edge of sweater. Starting at bottom right side, work 1 row single crochet along front edge to top, make 3 single crochets in corner to turn, continue single crochet to edge of Collar, join with a slip stitch, turn. Work another row of single crochet along front edge, making 4 buttonholes, starting about 4 inches (10 cm) from top, chain 1, and turn. [*To make buttonholes*: chain 2, skip 2 stitches.] Make another row of single crochet, do not turn. Work 1 row backward single crochet, end off. Starting at edge of Collar on Left Front, work border to correspond. Do not block. Sew buttons in place, tacking Belt down with buttons in back.

girl's dress-up cardigan

Girls' Sizes
Directions are for size 4. Changes for sizes 6 and 8 are in parentheses.

Materials
4 skeins (3.5 oz or 100 g each) Red Heart 4-ply Knitting Worsted by Coats & Clark, or any knitting worsted to give gauge—2 in Color A, 1 each in Colors B and C

Hook
Size 10½ or K

Gauge
3 stitches = 1 inch (2.5 cm)
To save time, take the time to check gauge.

Note: Body is worked in 1 piece to armhole.

Body
With size 10½ hook, chain 62 (66, 70).
Foundation row: Work 1 double crochet in 3rd chain from hook, 1 double crochet in each stitch across row [60, (64, 68) double crochets].
Row 1: Chain 2 to turn, skip the first stitch [chain 2 counts as the first double crochet], make 1 double crochet in each stitch to end of row.
  Repeat Row 1 for 6 (7, 8) inches (15, 16.3, 17.5 cm), or desired length to underarm. Do not break yarn.

Left Front
Chain 2 and turn, work 1 double crochet in each of the next 13 (14, 15) stitches, chain 2, and turn. Decrease 1 stitch arm side and repeat the decrease at the arm side, every row, 2 times more. Work even till armhole is 4 (4½, 5) inches (10, 11.3, 12.5 cm), ending at front edge. Slip stitch over 3 stitches, work across row. Continuing in pattern as established, decrease 1 stitch at neck edge, every row, 2 times. Work even till armhole is 5½ (6, 6½) inches (13.8, 15, 16.3 cm), end off.

Right Front
Join yarn 14 (15, 16) stitches in from other side and complete to correspond with Left Front, reversing all shaping.

Top Back Section
Skip 1 stitch at each underarm, work Back on 30 (32, 34) center stitches. Decrease 1 stitch each side, every row, 2 times. Work even till armhole is 5½ (6, 6½) inches (13.8, 15, 16.3 cm), end off.

Sleeves
Chain 22 (24, 26). Work in double crochet same as Back, increasing 1 stitch each side, every 3rd row, 3 (4, 5) times. Work even till 7½ (8, 8½) inches (18.8, 20, 21.3 cm), or 1 inch (2.5 cm) less than desired finished length. Slip stitch over 3 stitches, work to within 3 stitches of other side, chain 2, and turn. Continuing in pattern, decrease 1 stitch each side, every row, 5 (6, 7) times, end off.

Girl's Dress-Up Cardigan
The bands of this dress-up sweater are done in contrasting colors and can be coordinated with the colors in a little girl's wardrobe.

Finishing

Sew shoulder seams. Sew underarm seams on Sleeves and set in. Starting at bottom, about 5 inches over from corner, join Color B, work in single crochet to bottom right corner, make 3 single crochets in corner space, continue single crochet up right front to top corner, make 3 single crochets in corner, continue single crochet along top of neck, skipping every 8th stitch, make 3 single crochets in top left corner, continue down left front [be sure to pick up same amount of stitches that were picked up on right front], make 3 single crochets in bottom left corner, continue single crochet along bottom to where you started, join with a slip stitch, break Color B. Using Color A, then Color C, then Color A, work 3 more rows the same all around outside edge of jacket. Work same trim at bottom of Sleeves.

27

child's tennis sweater

Children's Sizes
Directions are for size 2. Changes for sizes 4 and 6 are in parentheses.

Materials
2 skeins (3.5 oz or 99.2 g each) Red Heart 4-ply Knitting Worsted by Coats & Clark, or any knitting worsted to give gauge—in Color A and small amounts in Colors B and C

Hooks	**Gauge**
Size 8 or H	2 stitches = 1 inch (2.5 cm)
Size 10½ or K	To save time, take the time to check gauge.

Back
With smaller hook, chain 10.
Foundation row: Work 1 single crochet from the back loop in 2nd chain from hook, 1 single crochet from the back loop in each stitch to end of row [9 (9, 9) single crochets].
Row 1: Chain 1 to turn, skip the first stitch [chain 1 counts as the first stitch], make 1 single crochet from the back loop in each stitch to end of row.

Repeat Row 1 for 38 (40, 42) rows [19 (20, 21) ridges], do not break yarn. Change to larger hook, and, working along top edge of piece just made, pick up 1 single crochet in each row [38 (40, 42) stitches]. Chain 2 to turn, work 1 single crochet in 2nd stitch from hook *1 double crochet in next stitch, 1 single crochet in next stitch, repeat from * across row, chain 2 to turn. Repeat the last row, working 2 rows each of Colors B and C, then continue in Color A till 10 (10½, 11) inches (25, 25.3, 27.5 cm), or desired length to underarm. Slip stitch across 3 stitches, work pattern to within 3 stitches of other side, chain 1, and turn. Continuing in pattern, decrease 1 stitch each side, every row, 2 times. Work even till armhole is 5½ (6, 6½) inches (13.8, 15, 16.3 cm), end off.

Front
Work same as Back till armhole. Start armhole shaping, and, at the same time, divide work in half, and work on Left Side only. Shape arm sides same as Back, and, at the same time, decrease 1 stitch at neck edge, every other row, till 6 (8, 8) stitches remain. Work to shoulder, end off.

Sleeves
With smaller hook, chain 10, and work same as Back for 22 rows. Change to larger hook and pick up 24 stitches along top edge. Work in pattern, increasing 1 stitch each side, every 2 inches (7.5 cm), 2 (3,. 4) times. Work even till Sleeve is 11 (12, 13) inches (27.5, 30, 32.5 cm), or desired length to underarm. Slip stitch over 3 stitches, work to within 3 stitches of other side, then, continuing in pattern, decrease 1 stitch each side, every row, 6 (7, 8) times. Work 1 (1, 2) row(s) even, then work 2 stitches together all across the next row, end off.

Child's Tennis Sweater
The tennis sweater is a perennial favorite of girls and boys alike. A combination stitch, which incorporates single and double crochet, creates the unusual texture.

Finishing

Sew shoulders, sew underarm seams, set in Sleeves. With smaller hook and Color B, work 1 row single crochet around neck. With Color C, work a 2nd row. Do not block.

woman's tweed coat

(See photograph in color section.)

Women's Sizes
Directions are for small size. Changes for medium and large sizes are in parentheses.

Materials
25 (26, 27) skeins (1⁷⁄₁₀ oz or 50 g each) Derby by Unger Yarns or any bulky yarn to give gauge

Hooks
Size 6 or G
Size 10½ or K

Gauge
2 single crochets or 2 double crochets = 1 inch (2.5 cm)
To save time, take the time to check gauge.

Pattern
Row 1: Single crochet across.
Row 2: Double crochet across.

Back
With larger hook, chain 53 (55, 57).
Foundation row: Work 1 double crochet in 3rd chain from hook, 1 double crochet in each chain to end of row [50 (52, 54) double crochets].
Row 1: Chain 1 to turn, skip the first stitch [chain 1 counts as the first stitch], make 1 single crochet in each stitch to end of row.
Row 2: Chain 3 to turn, skip the first stitch [chain 3 counts as the first double crochet], make 1 double crochet in each stitch to end of row.

Continue to repeat Rows 1 and 2 for pattern till 30 (31, 32) inches (75, 77.5, 80 cm) from the beginning, or desired length to underarm. Next row, slip stitch over 3 (3, 4) stitches, work to within 3 (3, 4) stitches of other side, chain, and turn. Continuing in pattern, decrease 1 stitch each side, every other row, 16 (18, 20) times. End off.

Left Front
Chain 30 (33, 36). Work same as Back till armhole. Shape arm sides as Back and, at the same time, when 13 (14, 15) decreases have been made, shape neck as follows: At front edge, slip stitch over 8 (8, 9) stitches, then decrease 1 stitch neck edge, every row, 3 (5, 5) times, end off.

Right Front
Work same as Left Front, reveresing arm side and neck shaping.

Sleeves
Chain 32 (34, 36). Work pattern same as Back till 16 (16½, 17) inches (40, 41.3, 42.5 cm), or desired length to underarm. Slip stitch over 3 (3, 4) stitches, work to within 3 (3, 4) stitches of other side,

30

chain, and turn. Continuing in pattern, decrease 1 stitch each side, every other row, 16 (18, 20) times, end off.

Collar
Chain 40 (42, 44). Work in pattern as Back for 5 inches (12.5 cm).

Pockets
Chain 16, work in pattern as Back for 6 inches (15 cm), end off.

Finishing
Sew seams. Set in Sleeves. Sew Collar in place, being sure to mark Center Back before sewing. Fold Collar in half to inside and stitch down. Work 1 row single crochet around Pockets and sew in place. With larger hook, starting at bottom of Right Front, work 1 row single crochet along front edge, working right up to the top and going through both thicknesses of Collar. Chain 1 and turn. Work a second row of single crochet, making 3 buttonholes starting just below Collar, and every 6 inches (15 cm) thereafter. [*To make buttonholes*: chain 2, skip 1 stitch.] At end of row, chain 1. Work a third row of single crochet, making 1 single crochet in each buttonhole space, end off. Starting at top of Left Front, work 3 rows single crochet along Left Front to correspond. Using the smaller hook, work 2 inches (5 cm) single crochet along bottom of sleeve, pulling in slightly, if necessary, to tighten cuff.

Women's Sizes
Directions are for size 10. Changes for sizes 12 and 14 are in parentheses.

Materials
5 (5, 6) skeins (3.5 oz or 100 g each) Germantown Knitting Worsted by Brunswick, or any worsted to give gauge

Hook
Wooden size 15
Knitting needles size 8

Gauge
2 stitches = 1 inch (2.5 cm)
To save time, take the time to check gauge.

Back
With size 15 wooden hook, chain 34 (36, 38).
Foundation row: Work 1 single crochet in each stitch to end of row.
Row 1: Chain 1 to turn, skip 2 stitches *make 1 single crochet, 1 half double crochet in next stitch, skip 1 stitch, repeat from * across row, end 1 single crochet in last stitch.
Row 2: Chain 1 to turn, make 1 single crochet and 1 half double crochet in each single crochet across row, skipping the half double

woman's lacy pullover
(See photograph in color section.)

crochets, end with 1 single crochet in top of turning chain.

Repeat Row 2 only, till 10 (11, 12) inches (25, 27.5, 30 cm), or 3 inches less than desired length to underarm. Slip stitch over 4 stitches work to within 4 stitches of other side, chain 1, and turn. Continuing in pattern, decrease 1 stitch each side, every other row, 2 times. Work even till armhole is 7 (7½, 8) inches (17.5, 18.8, 20 cm), end off.

Front
Work same as Back till armhole is 5 (5½, 6) inches (12.5, 13.8, 15 cm). Shape neck as follows: work across 10 stitches, chain 1, and turn. Working on these stitches only, decrease 1 stitch neck edge, every row, 4 times. Work even, if necessary, to shoulder, end off. Skip the center stitches, join yarn 10 stitches in from other side, and complete to correspond.

Sleeves
Chain 24 (26, 28). Work pattern same as Back till 15 (16, 17) inches (37.5, 40, 42.5 cm), or 3 inches (7.5 cm) less than desired length to underarm [allow for blousing of sleeve]. Slip stitch over 2 stitches, work to within 2 stitches of other side, chain 1, and turn. Continue in pattern till cap is 7 (7½, 8) inches (17.5, 18.8, 20 cm). On the next row, work 2 stitches together all across row, end off.

Knit Borders and Cuffs
For Back and Front, cast on 64, 68, 70 stitches. Knit 1, purl 1 in ribbing for 3 inches, bind off. For Sleeves, cast on 34 (36, 38) stitches, knit 1, purl 1 in ribbing for 3 inches (7.5 cm), bind off.

Finishing
Sew underarm seams, sew one shoulder. With knitting needle, right side of garment facing you, pick up 74 (76, 78) stitches around neck. Knit 1, purl 1 in ribbing for 2 inches (5 cm), bind off. Fold neckband in half to inside and stitch down. Sew remaining seams and set in Sleeves. Sew bottom Borders and Cuffs to sweater, easing fullness of body to Borders. Do not block.

woman's granny shawl
(See photograph in color section.)

Sizes
One size fits all.

Materials
6 skeins (3.5 oz or 100 g each) Germantown Knitting Worsted by Brunswick, or any knitting worsted to give gauge—1 skein each in Colors A, C, D, and E, and 2 skeins in Color B

Hook
Size 10½ or K

Gauge
1 cluster = 1 inch
To save time, take the time to check gauge.

Note: Shawl is worked from center outward, all in 1 piece.

Striping Pattern

Foundation row and Row 1 in Color A

10 rows in Color B	1 row in Color D
2 rows in Color A	2 rows in Color E
3 rows in Color C	1 row in Color B
2 rows in Color B	1 row in Color E
1 row in Color D	2 rows in Color B
2 rows in Color A	1 row in Color A
3 rows in Color B	1 row in Color B

Body

With size 10½ hook, chain 4, join with a slip stitch to form a circle.
Foundation row: Chain 4 [counts as 1 double crochet], work 1 double crochet, chain 1, 11 times in center of circle, join with a slip stitch to 3rd stitch of starting chain 4.
Row 1: Chain 3 [counts as 1 double crochet], make 2 more double crochets in same space [this counts as one-half of a corner], *chain 2, skip 3 double crochets, make 3 double crochets, chain 3, 3 double crochets all in next space [full corner]. Repeat from * twice, chain 2, skip 3 double crochets, make 3 double crochets in same space as you started, chain 3, and join with a slip stitch to top of starting chain 3 [this completes the final corner].
Row 2: Chain 3 [counts as 1 double crochet], make 2 more double crochets in same space [this counts as one-half of a corner], *chain 2, skip 3 double crochets, make 3 double crochets in next space, chain 2, make 3 double crochets, chain 3, 3 double crochets all in next space [full corner]. Repeat from * twice, chain 2, skip 3 double crochets, 3 double crochets in next space, chain 2, 3 double crochets in same space as you started, chain 3, join with a slip stitch to top of starting chain 3 [this completes the final corner].

Continue to work in Striping Pattern, keeping corners as established and always having 1 more group of 3 double crochets between each corner after each row. Do not block.

Men's Sizes

Directions are for size 36–38. Changes for sizes 40–42 and 44–46 are in parentheses.

Materials

9 (10, 11) skeins (3.5 oz or 100 g each) Germantown Knitting Worsted by Brunswick, or any knitting worsted to give gauge

Hooks

Size 10½ or K
Boye aluminum size N

man's shawl-collared jacket

(See photograph in color section.)

Gauge
2 single crochets = 1 inch (2.5 cm)
To save time, take the time to check gauge.

Note: Yarn is used double strand throughout.

Back
With larger hook, chain 39 (41, 43).
Foundation row: Work 1 single crochet in 2nd chain from hook, 1 single crochet in each stitch across row [38 (40, 42) single crochets].
Row 1: Chain 1, turn, skip the first stitch [chain 1 counts as the first stitch], work 1 single crochet in each stitch to end of row.

Repeat Row 1 till 16 (16½, 17) inches (40, 41.3, 42.5 cm) from beginning, or desired length to underarm. Slip stitch over 3 stitches, work to within 3 stitches of other side, chain, and turn. Continuing in pattern as established, decrease 1 stitch each side, every row, 3 times. Work even till armhole is 9½ (9½, 10) inches (23.8, 23.8, 25 cm), end off.

Left Front
Chain 22 (24, 26). Work same as Back to armhole. Shape arm side same as Back, and, *at the same time,* decrease 1 stitch at neck edge, every 3rd row. Continue in this manner till there are 8 (8, 9) stitches left. Work even to shoulder, end off.

Right Front
Work same as Left Front, reversing all armhole and neck shaping.

Sleeves
Chain 20 (22, 24). Work in single crochet same as Back, increasing 1 stitch each side, every 3 inches (7.5 cm), 5 (5, 6) times. Work even till 17 (17½, 18) inches (42.5, 43.8, 45 cm) from the beginning, or desired length to underarm. Slip stitch over 3 stitches, work to within 3 stitches of other side, chain, and turn. Continuing in pattern, decrease 1 stitch each side, every row, 8 (9, 10) times, work 2 rows even, end off.

Collar
With smaller hook, chain 7. Work in single crochet from the back loop till same length as Front to beginning of neck shaping. Mark 1 side for inside edge. Then, continuing in same pattern as established, increase 1 stitch at inside edge only, every row, 6 times. Continue working on all stitches till 30 inches (75 cm) from marker. Continue, decreasing 1 stitch same side, every row, 6 times. Work even till same length as other side, end off.

Pockets
Chain 15, work in single crochet same as Back for 6 inches (15 cm), end off.

Belt
Chain 52, work in single crochet same as Back for 4 rows, end off.

Finishing
Sew shoulders, sew underarm seams. Pin Collar at center back, at bottom, and at start of neck shaping, sew in place. Sew on Pockets. Do not block.

young woman's picot-edged jacket

(See photograph in color section.)

Young Women's Sizes
Directions are for size 10. Changes for sizes 12 and 14 are in parentheses.

Materials
6 (7, 7) skeins (1.7 oz or 50 g each) Fluffy Yarn by Unger, or any brushed yarn to give gauge
5 buttons

Hook
Size 10½ or K

Gauge
2 double crochets = 1 inch (2.5 cm)
To save time, take the time to check gauge.

Back
With size 10½ hook, chain 54 (57, 60).
Foundation row: Work 1 double crochet, chain 1, 1 double crochet in the 5th chain from hook [1 V stitch made], skip 2 chains, *work 1 V stitch in the next stitch, skip 2, repeat from * across row, ending the row with 1 double crochet in the last stitch [16 (17, 18) V stitches, 1 double crochet each side].
Row 1: Chain 3 to turn, make 1 V stitch in the chain-1 space of row below. Continue to make 1 V stitch in each chain-1 space across row, ending the row with 1 double crochet in the top of the turning chain.

Repeat Row 1 till 8 (9, 10) inches (20, 22.5, 25 cm) from the beginning. Slip stitch over 2 V stitches, then chain 3, and continue across the row to within 3 V stitches of other side, make 1 double crochet between the 3rd and 4th V stitch in from end. Continuing in pattern, decrease 1 stitch each side, every row, 2 times. [*To decrease:* eliminate half the V stitch each time.] Work even till armhole is 8 (8½, 9) inches (20, 21.3, 22.5 cm), end off.

Left Front
Chain 30 (33, 36). Work same as Back to armhole. Shape arm side as Back, and, at the same time, decrease 1 stitch at neck edges, every other row, till there are 3 V stitches left. Work even, if necessary, to shoulder, end off.

35

Right Front

Work same as Left Front, reversing all armhole and neck shaping.

Sleeves

Chain 22 (24, 26). Work pattern same as Back, increasing 1 stitch each side, every 3 inches (7.5 cm), 3 (4, 5) times. Be sure to form new patterns as stitches are increased. Work even till 14 (15, 16) inches (35, 37.5, 40 cm) from beginning, or desired length to underarm. Slip stitch over 3 stitches, then decrease 1 stitch each side, every other row, 2 times. Work even till cap of Sleeve is 6 (7, 7½) inches (15, 17.5, 18.8 cm). Next row, decrease each stitch across, end off.

Finishing

Sew shoulder seam and set in Sleeves. Sew underarm seams. Make picot edging as follows: starting at bottom right seam, work 1 row single crochet all around edges, making 3 single crochets in corners to turn. Join with a slip stitch to first stitch. Next row, *chain 3, make 1 single crochet in the base of the chain 3, skip 1 stitch, make 1 single crochet in the next stitch, repeat from * all around. Make same edging around armhole working over armhole seam. Make same edging around bottom of sleeve. Do not block. Sew buttons in place and button in open spaces of V stitches.

the "great granny" afghan

(See photograph in color section.)

Size

40 by 50 inches (100 by 125 cm)

Materials

12 skeins (3.5 oz or 100 g each) Germantown Knitting Worsted by Brunswick, or any knitting worsted to give gauge—8 skeins in Color A, 2 skeins in Color B, 2 skeins in Color C

Hook

Wooden size 15

Gauge

1 puff stitch = 1 inch (2.5 cm)
To save time, take the time to check gauge.

Note: Yarn is used double strand throughout.

Square   *(make 20)*

With Color B and size 15 hook, chain 4, join with a slip stitch to form a circle.
Row 1: Chain 4, (yarn over pick up a long loop) 4 times, yarn over and off all but last loop, yarn over and off 2 loops [puff stitch made], *chain 1, 1 puff in ring, repeat from * 6 times more [8 puff stitches in all], join with a slip stitch to top of chain 4, break Color A.
Row 2: Chain 4 with Color A, make 1 puff behind the space of chain 4 in row below, chain 1, skip 1 puff, *3 double crochets in next space, chain 1, skip 1 puff, make 1 puff, chain 3, 1 puff all in next

36

space, chain 1, skip 1 puff, repeat from * twice more, skip 1 puff, 3 double crochets in next space, chain 1, skip 1 puff, make 1 puff in same space as first puff, chain 3, join with a slip stitch to starting chain 4.

Row 3: Chain 4, make 1 puff in space behind chain 4 of row below *(chain 1, make 1 double crochet in next space) 4 times, chain 1, make 1 puff, chain 3, 1 puff all in next space, repeat from * twice more, (chain 1, 1 double crochet in next space) 4 times, chain 1, make 1 puff in same space as you started, chain 3, join with a slip stitch to top of starting chain 4.

Row 4: Work same as Row 2 except repeat between ()'s 5 times, end off Color A.

Row 5: Join Color B in any corner space, make 5 single crochets in corner space, *1 single crochet in each space to next corner, 5 single crochets in corner space, repeat from * 2 times, 1 single crochet in each of the next 6 spaces, join with a slip stitch to starting chain. Break Color B.

Row 6: Join Color C in the center stitch of any corner, make 3 single crochets in corner stitch, *1 single crochet in each stitch to next corner stitch, 3 single crochets in corner stitch, repeat from * 2 times, 1 single crochet in each of next single crochet, end with a slip stitch to first stitch, end off.

Finishing

Sew Squares together, 4 across, 6 down, sewing through the back loops of the last row of single crochet. With Color C, join in any corner stitch, chain 4, make 5 double crochets in same stitch, * make 1 double crochet in each stitch to next corner, make 6 double crochets in corner space, repeat from * twice, 1 double crochet in each remaining stitch, join with a slip stitch to top of starting chain.

Next row: Chain 8, *skip 2 stitches, make 1 single crochet in the next stitch, chain 8, repeat from * all around ending with a slip stitch to beginning stitch.

Next row: Work 8 single crochets in each chain-8 loop around, end off.

Do not block.

Men's Sizes

Directions are for small size. Changes for medium and large sizes are in parentheses.

Materials

10 (11, 12) skeins (3½ oz or 100 g each) Vail Homespun by Brunswick, or any bulky yarn to give gauge

Hook

Size 10½ or K
Boye aluminum size N

man's fisherman pullover

(See photograph in color section.)

Gauge
3 single crochets = 2 inches (5 cm)
To save time, take the time to check gauge.

Note: Yarn is used double strand throughout.
  Body of garment is worked from side over.

Pattern
Note: Each cable is completed before the next cable is begun. You will reverse directions twice to complete each separate cable.

Row 1 (right side): Single crochet in the first stitch, chain 3, skip 2 stitches, single crochet in the next stitch, turn work around, single crochet in each of the 3 chains, slip stitch in the single crochet before the chain was begun, turn [1 cable made]. Holding the cable toward you, work 1 single crochet in each of the 2 skipped stitches below the cable. *Chain 3, skip the single crochet where the previous chain is attached and the next 2 stitches, single crochet in the next stitch, turn. Single crochet in each of the 3 chains, slip stitch in the single crochet before chain was begun, turn. Holding the cable toward you, single crochet in the 2 skipped stitches, as before. Repeat from the * across row, ending with 1 single crochet in the last stitch [this is the same single crochet used to attach last chain 3], chain 1, turn.

Row 2: Single crochet in the first single crochet, single crochet in each of the next 2 single crochets behind first cable, * work 2 single crochets in first single crochet behind next cable, single crochet in next single crochet behind same cable. Repeat from * across, end the row by working a single crochet in first single crochet of previous row, chain 1, turn.

Diamond
Note: Row 1 of Pattern begins on wrong side.

Rows 1–3: Make 1 single crochet in each stitch across row, chain 1, and turn.

Row 4 (right side): Slip stitch in the first single crochet, chain 3. In Row 1, work a slip stitch around the post of the 4th single crochet as follows: Insert hook at right of post from front to back and again to front at left of stitch, draw a loop through and complete as a slip stitch, chain 3. In Row 3, skip 5 single crochets, slip stitch in next single crochet, *chain 3. In Row 1, skip 5 single crochets and slip stitch around the post of next single crochet, chain 3. In Row 3, skip 5 single crochets, slip stitch in next single crochet, repeat from * across. Do not turn, you will now be working from left to right across row just worked. **Chain 7, skip 5 single crochets, slip stitch in the same single crochet where the chain 3 was attached, working slip stitch over previous slipped stitch, repeat from ** across, ending last repeat by working a slip stitch in last single crochet of Row 3 [same stitch where first slip stitch of Row 4 was worked]. Chain 2. Do not turn.

Row 5 (right side): *Skip stitch used to anchor the chain 7, single crochet in each of next 5 single crochets that were skipped in Row

4, chain 1, repeat from * across, keeping each chain 7 to the right side of work, ending last repeat by working a single crochet in each of last 5 single crochets skipped in Row 4, single crochet in same single crochet used to attach last chain 3 in Row 4, chain 1, turn.

Row 6: Single crochet in each single crochet and in each chain-1 space across row, ending by working 1 single crochet in turning chain space, chain 1, turn.

Row 7: Single crochet in each single crochet across, chain 1, turn.

Row 8 (wrong side): Single crochet in each of first 3 single crochets, *attach chain 7 as follows: Insert hook in next single crochet and then in back ridge of center chain of the chain 7, pull up a loop, and complete as a single crochet. Single crochet in each of next 5 single crochets, repeat from * across, ending last repeat by working a single crochet in each of last 3 single crochets, chain 1, turn.

Back

With larger hook, chain 40 (41, 42).

Foundation row: Work 1 single crochet in the 2nd chain from hook and 1 single crochet in each stitch across row [39 (40, 41) single crochets].

Row 1: Chain 1 to turn, skip the first stitch [chain 1 counts as the first stitch], make 1 single crochet in each stitch across row.

Repeat Row 1 6 (8, 10) times more.

Row 8 (10, 12): Chain 1 to turn, skip 1 stitch, slip stitch from the front loop all across row.

Row 9 (11, 13): Chain 1 to turn, skip the first stitch, work 1 single crochet from the back loop all across row.

Rows 10 and 11 (12 and 13, 14 and 15): Work the 2 rows of Cable Pattern.

Row 12 (14, 16): Chain 1 and turn, skip the first stitch, work 1 single crochet in each stitch across row.

Row 13 (15, 17): Chain 1 turn, skip the first stitch, slip stitch in each stitch from the front loop, all across row.

Row 14 (16, 18): Chain 1 to turn, skip the first stitch, make 1 single crochet from the back loop in each stitch across row.

Rows 15–22 (17–24, 19–26): Work the 8 rows of Diamond Pattern.

Row 23 (25, 27): Repeat Row 13 (15, 17).

Row 24 (26, 28): Repeat Row 14 (16,18).

Rows 25 and 26 (27 and 28, 29 and 30): Repeat the 2 rows of Cable Pattern.

Rows 27–34 (29–36, 31–38): Repeat Row 1 1 (2, 4) time(s), end off.

Bottom border: With smaller hook, chain 10, work single crochet from the back loop for 46 (48, 50 rows), end off. Sew in place at bottom edge of Back section.

Front

Work same as Back.

Sleeves

Chain 28, work in single crochet for 28 (30, 30) rows, end off. Sew long ends together to form Sleeve. With larger hook, work 3 rows of single crochet around top of sleeve, picking up 1 stitch in each row [28 (30, 30) stitches], end off. *Make cuff as follows:* with smaller hook, chain 10, working in single crochet from the back loop, work 20 rows. Sew short ends of cuff together, sew to bottom of Sleeve, easing to fit.

Finishing

Sew shoulders 5 inches (12.5 cm) from each side edge, sew underarmseams, leaving 9 (9½, 9½) inches (22.5, 23.8 cm) for Sleeve. Pick up 28 (30, 30) stitches around each armhole [be sure to divide stitches equally on each side of shoulder seam], work 2 rows single crochet around armholes. Join top of sleeves to armhole, catching the back loops of the single crochet rows as you join. Work 2 rows singlecrochet around neck edge, pulling in slightly as you work. Do not block.

plaid afghan

(See photograph in color section.)

Size
50 by 50 inches (125 by 125 cm)

Materials
12 skeins (3.5 oz or 100 g each) Germantown Knitting Worsted by Brunswick, or any knitting worsted to give gauge—4 skeins each in Colors A, B, and C

Hook
Wooden size 15

Gauge
1½ double crochets = 1 inch (2.5 cm)
To save time, take the time to check gauge.

Note: Yarn is used double strand throughout.

First Strip *(make 3)*
With Color A and size 15 hook, chain 18.
Foundation row: Work 1 double crochet in 4th chain from hook, 1 double crochet in each chain thereafter [15 double crochets].
Row 1: Chain 3 to turn, skip the first stitch [chain 3 counts as the first double crochet], make 1 double crochet in each stitch to end of row.
   *Repeat Row 1, working colors as follows:
1 more row in Color A   2 rows Color B and
2 rows in Color B   3 rows Color A
2 rows Color A

   Still continuing in double crochet, work 12 rows of Color C, 2 rows of Color A, then repeat from * till 60 rows have been worked in all, end off.

Second Strip *(make 2)*
Work same as First Strip alternating colors as follows:
*3 rows in Color C

2 rows in Color B   5 rows in Color B
2 rows in Color C   2 rows in Color C and
2 rows in Color B   5 rows in Color B
3 rows in Color C
   Repeat from * till 60 rows have been worked, end off.

Finishing
Sew strips together starting with First Strip. Join Color C in 1 corner, work 1 row single crochet all around edges, making 3 single crochets in each corner to turn. Chain 3, (yarn over and pick up a long loop) 3 times in the next stitch [puff stitch made], chain 1, skip 1, *puffstitch in the next stitch, chain 1, skip 1, repeat from * to first corner stitch, make 1 puff, chain 3, 1 puff all in the corner stitch, continue to make 1 puff stitch, chain 1 in each stitch to corner, make 1 puff chain 3, 1 puff all in corner stitches, end with slip stitch to startingchain, end off. Do not block.

woman's nubby tunic
(See photograph in color section.)

Women's Sizes
Directions are for small size. Changes for medium and large sizes in parentheses.

Materials
12 (13, 14) skeins (2 oz or 56.7 g each) Nubs and Slubs by Stanley Berocco
6 (6, 7) skeins (2 oz or 56.7 g each) Donegal Tweed Homespun by Tahki Imports Ltd., or any nubby yarn to give gauge

Hook
Wooden size 15

Gauge
2 single crochets = 1 inch (2.5 cm)

Note: Yarn is used double strand (1 strand of each kind) held together throughout.

Back
With size 15 hook, chain 37 (39, 41).
Foundation row: Work 1 single crochet in each chain thereafter [36, 38, 40 single crochets].
Row 1: Chain 1 to turn, skip the first stitch [chain 1 counts as the first stitch], make 1 single crochet in each stitch to end of row.
   Repeat Row 1 till Back measures 15 (16, 17) inches (39, 41.5, 44 cm), or desired length to underarm. Slip stitch over the first 2 stitches, work single crochet to within 2 stitches of end of row. Do not work the last 2 stitches, chain 1, and turn. Continuing in pattern as established, work till armhole is 7 (7½, 8) inches (17.5, 19, 20 cm), end off.

Front
Work same as Back.

Sleeves

Sew shoulders 2½ (3, 3½) inches (6, 7.5, 9 cm) from each side. Starting at bind-off, with right side facing you, work 14 (15, 16) single crochets from armhole to shoulder, work 14 (15, 16) single crochets from shoulder to underarm. Work the Sleeve in single crochet as Back for 19 (19½, 20) inches (47.5, 49, 50 cm), end off. Work other Sleeve to correspond.

Twisted Cord Belt

Cut 8 pieces of yarn, each 5 times the desired finished length of Belt. Fold the strands in half, anchoring one end over a doorknob, then twist the strands over and over, until tightly twisted. Bring both ends together and allow to twist into cord. Tie securely, add tassels.

Finishing

Sew underarm seams, leaving 5 inches open at bottom for slits. Turn back 3 inches (7.5 cm) for cuffs. Do not block.

To make tassels, wrap yarn 15 times around a 5-inch piece of cardboard. Tie one end leaving about 10 inches of yarn on each side of knot that you have just made. Cut the other end of tassels. Join to the end of Belt with the long ends that you have left. Do not cut ends. Let them become part of tassel. Now take a separate piece of yarn and wrap it around and tie about ½ inch down from top. Trim bottom of tassel evenly.

puff-stitched crib blanket

(See photograph in color section.)

Size
32 by 36 inches

Materials
8 skeins (3.5 oz or 99.2 g each) Red Heart 4-ply Knitting Worsted by Coats & Clark, or any knitting worsted to give gauge—6 skeins in Color A, 1 each in Colors B and C

Hook
Boye aluminum size N

Gauge
2 stitches = 1 inch (2.5 cm)
To save time, take the time to check gauge.

Note: Yarn is used double strand throughout.
Contrasting colors are woven in after blanket is complete.

Blanket
With size N hook, chain 73 stitches loosely.
Foundation row: Work 1 double crochet in 3rd stitch from hook, 1 double crochet in each stitch across row.
Row 1: Chain 3 to turn, skip first double crochet, * 1 double crochet

in next double crochet, chain 3. Now, working over the bar of the double crochet just made, (yarn over, pick up a long loop) 3 times, yarn over and pull through all but last loop, yarn over and pull through remaining 2 loops, skip 1 stitch, repeat from *across row, ending with 1 double crochet in the last stitch.

Row 2: Chain 3 * make 2 double crochets in loop made by chain 3 [above puff], repeat from * across row, ending with 1 double crochet in top of the turning chain.

Repeat Rows 1 and 2 till 33 inches (82.5 cm), ending with Row 1, end off.

Finishing

Alternating Colors B and C, used 4 strand, weave in and out of the top of each double crochet row. With Color B, work 1 row single crochet around entire outer edge, making 3 single crochets in each corner to turn. Work another row with Color C, and another with Color A. End off, weave in ends. Do not block.

baby's sacque and hat

(See photograph in color section.)

Infants' Sizes

Directions are for size 9 months. Changes for sizes 18 months and 2 years are in parentheses.

Materials

2 skeins (3.5 oz or 100 g each) Red Heart 4-ply Knitting Worsted by Coats & Clark or any knitting worsted to give gauge—1 skein eachin Colors A and B
5 buttons

Hook	**Gauge**
Size 8 or H	3 stitches = 1 inch (2.5 cm)
	To save time, take the time to check gauge.

Note: Sweater is a raglan sleeve, worked from the top down.

Yoke

sacque

With size 8 hook and Color A, chain 57 (57, 61).

Foundation row: Work 1 double crochet in 2nd chain from hook, 1 double crochet in each chain thereafter [56 (56, 60) double crochets].

Row 1: Chain 2 to turn, skip the first stitch [chain 1 counts as the first double crochet], make 1 double crochet from the back loop in each of the next 8 (8, 9) stitches, make 1 double crochet, chain 1, 1 double crochet all in the next stitch [corner stitch made]. Make 1 double crochet from the back loop in each of the next 8 stitches, 1 corner stitch in next stitch, 1 double crochet from the back loop

43

in each of the next 18 (18, 20) stitches, 1 corner stitch in the next stitch, 1 double crochet from the back loop in each of the next 8 stitches, 1 corner stitch in the next stitch, 1 double crochet from the back loop in the last 9 (9, 10) stitches.

Row 2: Chain 2 to turn, make 1 double crochet from the back loop in the 2nd stitch and each stitch to corner space, make 1 double crochet, chain 1, 1 double crochet all in corner space. *Make 1 double crochet in the back loop of each stitch to next corner space, 1 double crochet, chain 1, 1 double crochet all in corner space, repeat from * two times more, 1 double crochet in each stitch to end of row, 1 double crochet in top of turning chain.

Repeat Row 2 3 (4, 5) times more with Color A, 2 times more with Color B. This ends Yoke, do not break yarn. Chain 2, turn, work in double crochet from the back loop to the first corner stitch, chain 2, skip the next section for Sleeve, and continue in double crochet from the back loop across the Back, chain 2, skip the next Sleeve, continue in pattern across Front. Chain 2, turn, continuing in pattern as established. Work the entire body sections as 1 piece for 10 (11, 12) rows more. Work 1 row single crochet. Chain 1, turn, work 1 more row single crochet, end off.

Sleeves

Joining yarn on the chain-2 at underarm, work around Sleeve, picking up every stitch, chain 2, and turn, working back and forth on Sleeve. Work pattern for 10 (11, 12) rows more. Work 1 row single crochet, decreasing every 5th stitch. Chain 1, turn, work 2 more rows single crochet.

Finishing

Sew underarm seam. Make trim as follows: starting at bottom right side, work 1 row single crochet along Right Front, make 3 single crochets in corner to turn, continue along neckline, make 3 single crochets in corner to turn, continue along Left Front, chain 1, turn. Make another row of single crochet, making 5 buttonholes evenly spaced on right side for girls, on left side for boys. [*To make buttonholes:* chain 2, skip 1 stitch. On 3rd row, make 1 single crochet in the buttonhole space.] Chain 1 turn, make a 3rd row of single crochet. At the end of the 3rd row, do not break yarn. Continue along bottom edge with a row of single crochet, end off.

hat **Body**

Chain 54 (56, 58).

Rows 1–6: Work in double crochet from the back loop.

Row 7: Chain 2, turn, work *1 double crochet from the back loop in each of the next 6 stitches, decrease over the next 2 stitches, repeat from * across row.

Repeat the decrease row every row till 12 stitches remain, end off leaving a long end for sewing. Gather top, sew side seam. Fold 2 rows up at bottom for brim.

Earlaps

Starting 8 stitches over from seam, pick up 8 (9, 10) stitches. Work in pattern, decreasing 1 stitch each side, every row, till 2 stitches remain, end off. Starting 8 stitches over from other side of seam, make another Earlap to correspond. Work 1 row single crochet in Color B at top of brim. Add pom-pom, and chain for ties. Join Color A to point of Earlap and work chain stitch for 10 inches, end off.

Girls' Sizes

Directions are for size 6. Changes for sizes 8 and 10 are in parentheses.

Materials

10 (11, 12) skeins (1.7 oz or 50 g each) Fluffy Yarn by Unger, or any brushed yarn to give gauge

Hooks
Size 10½ or K

Gauge
1 shell = 1 inch (2.5 cm)
To save time, take the time to check gauge.

girl's sweater coat
(See photograph in color section.)

Note: Yarn is used double strand throughout.

Back

With size 10½ hook, chain 30 (32, 34) loosely.
Foundation row: In 2nd chain from hook, make 1 single crochet, chain 1, 1 single crochet, skip 1 chain *make 1 single crochet, chain 1, 1 single crochet all in the next stitch, skip 1 chain, repeat from * across row, end 1 single crochet in last stitch [14 (15, 16) shells].
Row 1: Chain 2 to turn, work 1 single crochet, chain 1, 1 single crochet all in the first chain-1 space [1 shell made], continue to make 1 shell in each chain-1 space across row, ending row with 1 double crochet in the top of the turning chain.
Repeat Row 1 till 13 (14, 15) inches (32.5, 35, 37.5 cm). Slip stitch over 1 shell pattern, chain 2, continue shell pattern across row to within 1 shell of other side, chain 2, and turn. Work even till armhole is 5½ (6, 6½) inches (13.8, 15, 16.3 cm), end off.

Left Front

Chain 16 (18, 20). Work same as Back to armhole. At armhole, slip stitch over 1 shell pattern, work across row. Chain 2, turn. Keeping front edges even, work till armhole is same as Back to shoulder, ending at front edge. Chain 2 and turn. Work pattern over 4 (4, 5) shells, chain 2, and turn. Working on these 4 (4, 5) shells only, continue for 4 (4½, 5) inches (10, 11.3, 12.5 cm). [This section becomes the shawl collar.]

Right Front

Work same as Left Front, reversing armhole and collar shaping.

Sleeves

Sew shoulder seams. With right side facing you, start at underarm, bind off. Pick up 22 (24, 26) stitches along armhole to other side. Be sure to divide stitches equally. Work in shell pattern for 10 (11, 12) inches (25, 27.5, 30 cm), end off.

Belt

Chain 4, work 1 shell pattern for 44 (46, 46) inches (110, 115, 115 cm), end off.

Finishing

Sew underarm seams, seam collar at center back, sew to back of neck. Starting at Left Front edge, wrong side facing you, and at armhole level, work 1 row single crochet all around collar to other side, do not turn. Work 1 row single crochet backwards around stitches just made, do not break yarn. Turn garment with right side facing you, and work 1 row single crochet down along Left Front to bottom. Make 3 single crochets in corner to turn, continue single crochet along bottom edge, make 3 single crochets in corner to turn, continue up Right Front to edge of collar. Join with a slip stitch, end off. Do not block.

little girl's bulky coat

(See photograph in color section.)

Toddlers' Sizes

Directions are for size 2 Changes for sizes 3 and 4 are in parentheses.

Materials

14 (16, 18) skeins (1$7/10$ oz or 50 g each) Derby by Unger Yarns, or any bulky yarn to give gauge
6 buttons

Hooks

Boye aluminum size N

Gauge

1½ single crochets = 1 inch (2.5 cm)
To save time, take the time to check gauge.

Note: Yarn is used double strand throughout.

Back

With size N hook, chain 21 (23, 25).
Foundation row: Work 1 single crochet in 2nd chain from hook, 1 single crochet in each chain thereafter [20 (22, 24) single crochets].

Row 1: Chain 1 to turn, skip the first stitch [chain 1 counts as the first stitch], make 1 single crochet in each stitch to end of row.

Repeat Row 1 till Back measures 11 (11½, 12) inches (27.5, 28.8, 30 cm), or desired length to underarm. Slip stitch over 2 stitches, work to within 2 stitches of other side, chain 1, and turn. Work in pattern, decreasing 1 stitch each side, every other row, 1 (2, 2) time(s). Work even till armhole is 5½ (6, 6½) inches (13.8, 15, 16.3 cm), end off.

Left Front

Chain 11 (12, 13). Work same as Back to armhole. At arm side, slip stitch over 2 stitches, then decrease 1 stitch arm side, every other row, 1 (2, 2) time(s). Work even till armhole is 3½ (4, 5) inches (8.8, 10, 11.3 cm), ending at front edge. Slip stitch over 2 stitches, work across row. Continue in pattern, decreasing 1 stitch at neck edge, every row, 2 (2, 3) times. Work even to shoulder, end off.

Right Front

Work same as Left Front, reversing all shaping.

Sleeves

Chain 16 (17, 18). Work pattern same as Back for 10 (11, 12) inches (25, 27.5, 30 cm), or desired length to underarm, allowing 2 inches (5 cm) for turn-back cuff. Slip stitch over 2 stitches, work to within 2 stitches of other side, chain, and turn. Continue in pattern, decreasing 1 stitch each side, every row, 8 (9, 10) times, end off.

Collar

Chain 21 (21, 22). Work pattern for 3 inches (7.5 cm), end off. Work 1 row single crochet around 3 sides of Collar.

Pockets   *(make 2)*

Chain 8, work pattern for 4 inches (10 cm), end off.

Finishing

Sew shoulders and underarm seams. Sew sleeves and set in place. Sew on Pockets. Sew on Collar, centering Back, and having edges of Collar 1 inch (2.5 cm) in from each front edge. Starting at Top Left Front, next to Collar, work 1 row single crochet along front and bottom edges, making 3 single crochets in each corner to turn. Sew buttons in place, button in the open space between stitches. Do not block.

girl's tweed vest

(See photograph in color section.)

Girls' Sizes
Directions are for size 8. Changes for sizes 10 and 12 are in parentheses.

Materials
7 (8, 9) skeins (2 oz or 56.7 g each) Multiglo by Stanley Berocco, or any yarn to give gauge

Hook   **Gauge**
Size N   2 double crochets = 1 inch (2.5 cm)
         To save time, take the time to check gauge.

Note: Yarn is used double strand throughout.
  Vest is made in 1 piece.

Back and Fronts   *(up to armhole)*
With size N hook, chain 43 (47, 51).
Foundation row: Work 1 double crochet in 4th chain from hook, 1 double crochet in each chain thereafter [40 (44, 48) double crochets].
Row 1: Chain 3 to turn, skip the first stitch [chain 3 counts as 1 double crochet], make 1 double crochet in each stitch to end of row, 1 stitch in top of turning chain 3.
  Repeat Row 1 till 11 (12, 13) inches (28.5, 31, 33.5 cm), or desired length to underarm.

Left Front   *(from armhole to shoulder)*
Continuing as established, work across first 9 (10, 11) stitches, chain 3, turn. Working on this section only, decrease 1 stitch at arm side and front side, every other row, 2 times. Then decrease 1 stitch at front side only 1 (2, 3) time(s) more. Work even till armhole is 8 (8½, 9) inches (20.5, 22, 23 cm), end off.

Right Front   *(from armhole to shoulder)*
Join yarn 9 (10, 11) stitches in from other side, work to correspond to Left Front.

Back   *(from armhole to shoulder)*
Join yarn 2 stitches over from Left Front. Work in pattern to within 2 stitches of other Front, chain 3, turn. Continue in pattern as established, decreasing 1 stitch each side of Back section, every other row, 2 times. Work even till same as Front sections, end off.

Finishing
Sew shoulder seams. Join yarn at bottom, in line with underarm, and work 1 row of single crochet around entire outside edge of garment, making 3 single crochets in each bottom corner to turn. Join with a slip stitch to starting chain, end off. Work 1 row single crochet around armholes. Using yarn double strand, chain 70 (75, 80) for tie. Weave tie in and out of double crochet at waistline. Do not block.

48

Woman's Tweed Coat *(see directions on page 30)* The interesting texture of this coat is created by combining a bulky tweed yarn with simple single and double crochet rows.

Woman's Lacy Pullover *(see directions on page 31)* The knitted collar, waist-band, and cuffs of this lacy pullover set off the delicate stitch nicely.

Woman's Granny Shawl *(see directions on page 32)* This simple shawl is actually one giant granny square. It is super quick and easy to make.

Man's Shawl-Collared Jacket *(see directions on page 33)* The deep shawl collar, pockets, and belt are interesting features of this easy-to-make ribbed-look jacket.

Young Woman's Picot-Edged Jacket *(see directions on page* 35) This little jacket, cropped short, with a dainty picot edge is a natural for topping off pleated skirts or jeans.

Man's Fisherman Pullover *(see directions on page 37)* Fisherman crochet stitches are not the simplest ones to master, but the results are well worth the effort.

The "Great Granny" Afghan *(see directions on page* 36) Granny afghans have been around for ages, but this version, made with a double strand of knitting worsted yarn and a large wooden hook, is truly a "great granny."

Plaid Afghan *(see directions on page 40)* This unusual afghan is made in strips, the colors changed in such a way as to create the plaid effect. The stitch is a simple double crochet.

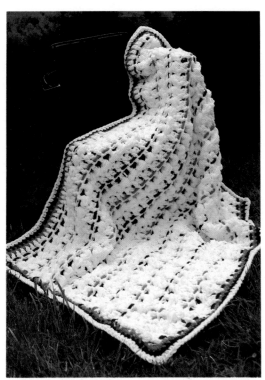

Woman's Nubby Tunic *(see directions on page 41)* Done in a simple single crochet stitch, this lovely tunic is set off by a twisted cord belt.

Puff-Stitched Crib Blanket *(see directions on page 42)* This puff-stitched blanket is made with a double strand of knitting worsted and a large crochet hook. The puff stitch works up very quickly.

Girl's Sweater Coat *(see directions on page 45)* The soft, fluffy yarn used to make this coat will make any little girl feel like a princess.

Baby's Sacque and Hat *(see directions on page 43)* This sacque is made in one piece from the neckline down. With little finishing required, it is quick and easy to make.

Toddler's Hooded Sweatshirt *(see directions on page 49)* The sweatshirt is a favorite among every age group, boy or girl. This one is crocheted in a jiffy, using a simple double crochet stitch and knitting worsted yarn.

Toddler's Striped-Yoked Cardigan and Hat *(see directions on page 50)* Adding bright, colored stripes is one way to brighten up a child's sweater. The simple pattern is fun and easy to do.

Little Girl's Bulky Coat *(see directions on page 46)* This coat is made entirely of single crochet in a beautiful nubby yarn, used double strand, on a very large hook. It is perfect for the first months of Fall.

Girl's Tweed Vest *(see directions on page 48)* Girls love to feel grown up, and this little vest is sure to please them. Made with an interesting yarn used double strand, the vest is quick and easy to make.

Toddlers' Sizes

Directions are for size 2. Changes for sizes 3 and 4 are in parentheses.

Materials

2 skeins (3.5 oz or 100 g each) Red Heart 4-ply Yarn by Coats & Clark, or any knitting worsted to give gauge—1 skein each in Colors A and B

Hook   **Gauge**
Size 8 or H   3 stitches = 1 inch (2.5 cm)
               To save time, take the time to check gauge.

Note: This garment is worked in an unusual method. The sleeve is made in 1 piece with the Back and the Fronts, and it is worked from the shoulders down.

Back and Sleeve

With size 8 hook, starting at shoulder back, chain 100 (106, 112).
Foundation row: Work 1 single crochet in 2nd chain from hook, 1 single crochet in each chain thereafter [99 (105, 111) single crochets].
Row 1: Chain 1 to turn, skip the first stitch [chain 1 counts as the first stitch] make 1 single crochet from the back loop in each of the next 6 stitches, then make 1 double crochet from the back loop in each of the next 85 (91, 97) stitches, 1 single crochet from the back loop in each of the last 7 stitches.
Row 2: Chain 1 to turn, skip the first stitch [chain 1 counts as the first stitch], make 1 single crochet from the back loop in each stitch across row.

Repeat Rows 1 and 2 6 (8, 10) times more, end off. Skip 33 (35, 37) stitches from end, join yarn, and work double crochet on the center 33 (35, 37) stitches from the back loop, continuing in pattern, alternating a row of single crochet and a row of double crochet from the back loop. Work this center Back section for 15 (17, 19) rows more. Next row, work in single crochet, decreasing 1 stitch every 5th stitch. Repeat the decrease row 2 times more. Work 1 more row single crochet, end off.

Left Front Top Section

Chain 50 (103, 106). Work same as Back till 8 (10, 12) rows are completed. Set aside.

Right Front Top Section

Work as Left Front.

Fronts

Skip 33 (35, 37) stitches from outside edge and work to end of one Front, then continue along other Front, leaving 33 (35, 37) stitches not worked at end. Complete for Back.

Hood

Sew shoulder seams. With right side facing you, starting at front opening, work in double crochet, picking up stitches along neckline, increasing every 10th stitch. Now work in pattern, alternating single and double crochet from the back loop for 16 (20, 24) rows more, end off.

Pocket

Chain 15, work in pattern, increasing 1 stitch each side, every row, 4 (5, 5) times. Continue in pattern for 4 (5, 6) rows more, end off.

Finishing

Sew underarm seams. Sew top of Hood. Work 1 row single crochet, 1 row backward single crochet around Pocket, using Color B. Sew Pocket in place. Starting at bottom of neck opening, work 1 row single crochet and 1 row backward single crochet all around opening and Hood, using Color B. Make pom-pom in Color B for Hood, sew on. Do not block.

toddler's striped-yoked cardigan and hat

(See photograph in color section.)

Toddlers' Sizes

Directions are for size 1. Changes for size 2 and 3 are in parentheses.

Materials

4 skeins (3.5 oz or 99.2 g each) Red Heart 4-ply Knitting Worsted by Coats & Clark, or any knitting worsted to give gauge—2 skeins in Color A, 1 skein each in Colors B and C

Hook
Size 10½ or K

Gauge
2 stitches = 1 inch (2.5 cm)
To save time, take the time to check gauge.

cardigan

Back

With Color A and size 10½ hook, chain 34 (38, 42).
Foundation row: Work 1 single crochet in 3rd chain from hook, *1 double crochet in next stitch, 1 single crochet in next stitch, repeat from * across.
Row 1: Chain 2 with Color B, skip the first stitch [chain 2 counts as a double crochet], make 1 single crochet in the next double crochet, *1 double crochet in the next single crochet, 1 single crochet in the next double crochet, repeat from * across row. Break Color B, join Color C.
Row 2: Repeat Row 1, break Color C.
Row 3: Chain 2 with Color A and repeat Row 1.
Repeat Row 1, twice making a stripe each in Color B and Color C, then continue in Color A till 7 (8, 9) inches (18.8, 20, 22.5 cm) from beginning. Slip stitch over 3 stitches, work to within 3 stitches

of other side. Continue in pattern as established, working 1 row in Color A, and 1 row each of Colors B and C for the entire Yoke, decreasing 1 stitch each side, every row, 3 times. Work even in pattern till armhole is 4½ (5, 5½) inches (11.3, 12.5, 13.8 cm), end off.

Left Front
With Color A and size 10½ hook, chain 17 (19, 21). Work same as Back till armhole. Shape arm side and Yoke same as Back. Work till armhole is 3½ (4, 4½) inches (8.8, 10, 11.3 cm), end at front edge. Slip stitch over 3 stitches, then decrease 1 stitch front edge, every row, 3 times. Work even to shoulder, end off.

Right Front
Work same as Left Front, reverse all shaping.

Sleeves
With Color A and size 10½ hook, chain 14 (16, 18). Work striping pattern as bottom Back, then increase 1 stitch each side. Continuing the rest of Sleeve in Color A, increase 1 stitch each side, every 1½ inches, 2 (3, 4) times more. Work even till Sleeve is 8 (9, 10) inches (20, 22.5, 25 cm). Slip stitch over 3 stitches, work to within 3 stitches of other side, then decrease 1 stitch each side, every other row, for 4 (4½, 5) inches (10, 11.3, 12.5 cm), end off.

Finishing
Sew shoulder seams, sew underarm seams, set in Sleeves. Starting at bottom right corner, with Color A, work 3 rows single crochet around front and neck edges, making 5 buttonholes evenly spaced on 2nd row. [*To make buttonholes:* chain 2, skip 1 stitch. On 3rd row, make 1 single crochet in buttonhole space.] Do not block.

With Color A and size 10½ hook, chain 40 (42, 44). Work stitch and striping pattern same as Back, then, continuing in Color A only, work 4 (4½, 5) inches (10, 11.3, 12.5 cm) more, end off. Joining yarn to work center 12 (14, 14) stitches only, continue on this section for same length as side pieces, end off.

hat

Finishing
Sew back seams. Fold stripe pattern back at front to make band. Working through both thicknesses at band, work 1 row of single crochet along bottom of Hat, skipping every 5th stitch. At end of row, chain 30 [tie], turn, work 1 row single crochet on chain just made, continue with single crochet along bottom of Hat, chain 30 at end of row [Tie]. Work 1 row single crochet on chain just made, work 1 more row single crochet along bottom of Hat, end off. Join yarn at bottom right corner, work 1 row single crochet along front of Hat, chain 1, do not turn, work 1 row backward single crochet on same stitches, end off. Do not block.

Child's Hat and Scarf Set
With five skeins of yarn, a large wooden crochet hook, and about three hours of time, you can make this beautiful hat and scarf.

Children's Sizes

Directions are for small size. Changes for medium and large sizes are in parentheses.

Materials

4 (5, 5) skeins (2 oz or 57 g each) Aspen by Brunswick, or any bulky yarn to give gauge—2 (3, 3) skeins in Color A, 1 each in Colors B and C

Hook

Wooden size 15

Gauge

1½ stitches = 1 inch (2.5 cm)
To save time, take the time to check gauge.

child's hat and scarf set

hat

With size 15 wooden hook, and Color A, chain 30 (32, 34).
Foundation row: Work 1 single crochet in 2nd chain from hook, and 1 single crochet from the back loop in each chain thereafter [29 (31, 33) single crochets].
Row 1: Chain 1 to turn, skip the first stitch [chain 1 counts as the first stitch], make 1 single crochet from the back loop in each stitch to end of row.

Repeat Row 1 8 times more. Break Color A, join Color B, work 1 row single crochet from the back loop. Next row, *work single crochet from the back loop on next 6 stitches, decrease 1 stitch, repeat from * across row. Still continuing with Color B, repeat Row 1 twice more, then repeat decrease row, decreasing every 5th stitch. Break Color B, join Color C, work as follows:

Row 1: Work in single crochet from the back loop, decreasing every 4th stitch.
Row 2: Work in single crochet from the back loop, decreasing every 3rd stitch.
Rows 3 and 4: Repeat Rows 1 and 2, decreasing every 3rd, then every 2nd stitch. Work 1 row even, end off. Cut yarn, leaving a long end for sewing. Gather top sew back seam. Add pom-pom.

scarf

With size 15 hook and Color C, chain 65. Working in single crochet pattern from the back loop, same as Hat, work as follows:
2 rows in Color C
2 rows in Color B
8 rows in Color A
2 rows in Color B
2 rows in Color C

End off, add fringe. Do not block.

woman's hat and scarf set

Materials for Hat and Scarf
9 skeins (2 oz or 57 g each) Aspen Bulky by Brunswick, or any bulky yarn to give gauge—4 skeins in Color A, 2 skeins in Color B, and3 skeins in Color C

Hook
Size 10½ or K

Gauge
2½ double crochets = 1 inch (2.5 cm)
To save time, take the time to check gauge.

hat

Striping Pattern
2 rows in Color A
2 rows in Color B
2 rows in Color C

Body
With size 10½ hook and Color C, chain 39.
Foundation row: Work 1 double crochet in 3rd chain from hook, 1 double crochet in each of the next 30 chains, 1 single crochet in each of next 5 chains.
Row 1: Chain 1 to turn, skip the first stitch [chain 1 counts as first stitch], 1 single crochet in the next 4 single crochets, 1 double crochet in each double crochet to end of row.
Row 2: Starting with Color A, start working Striping Pattern. Chain 3 to turn, skip the first stitch [chain 3 counts as first double crochet], 1 double crochet in each of next 30 stitches, 1 single crochet in each of next 5 stitches.
 Repeat Row 2, being sure to follow Striping Pattern, until 18 rows have been worked, end off.

Finishing
Fold Hat in half so that stripes are vertical, sew seam, do not break thread. Gather top together, and tie securely. Add pom-pom to top of hat, if desired. Do not block.

scarf

Striping Pattern
2 rows in Color C
2 rows in Color A
2 rows in Color B
2 rows in Color A
2 rows in Color C

Woman's Hat and Scarf Set

Hat and scarf sets like this one make great chill chasers. Very bulky yarn and a large crochet hook make them very quick and easy to make. Make a set for everyone on your gift-giving list and then one for yourself, as well.

Body

With size 10½ hook and Color C, chain 163.

Foundation row: Work 1 double crochet in 3rd chain from hook, 1 double crochet in each chain thereafter [160 double crochets].

Row 1: Chain 3 to turn, skip the first stitch [chain 3 counts as first double crochet], *1 double crochet in the next stitch, repeat from * across row.

Repeat Row 1, working in Striping Pattern 8 times, end off.

Finishing

Fringe ends. [*To make fringe:* wrap yarn around an 8-inch (20-cm) piece of cardboard, cut 1 end, draw pieces through ends of scarf with a crochet hook, and knot.] Do not block.

Young Woman's V-Stitched Vest
A welcome addition to any wardrobe, this little vest can literally be made in one night. It makes a great last-minute gift.

Young Women's Sizes

Directions are for size 8. Changes for sizes 10 and 12 are in parentheses.

Materials

4 (5, 5) skeins (1.7 oz or 50 g each) Fluffy Yarn by Unger, or any brushed yarn to give gauge

Hook
Size 10 or J

Gauge
2 double crochets = 1 inch (2.5 cm)
To save time, take the time to check gauge.

Back

With size 10½ hook, chain 54 (57, 60).
Foundation row: Work 1 double crochet, chain 1, 1 double crochet in the 5th chain from hook [1 V stitch made], skip 2 chains, *work 1 V stitch in the next stitch, skip 2, repeat from * across row, ending the row with 1 double crochet in the last stitch [16 (17, 18) V stitches, 1 double crochet each side].
Row 1: Chain 3 to turn, make 1 V stitch in the chain-1 space of row below. Continue to make 1 V stitch in each chain-1 space across row, ending the row with 1 double crochet in the top of the turning chain.

Repeat Row 1 till 8 (9, 10) inches (20, 22.5, 25 cm) from the beginning. Slip stitch over 2 V stitches, then chain 3, and continue across the row to within 3 V stitches of other side. Make 1 double crochet between the 3rd and 4th V stitch in from end. Continuing in pattern, decrease 1 stitch each side, every row, 2 times. [*To decrease:* eliminate half the V stitch each time.] Work even till armhole is 8 (8½, 9) inches (20, 21.3, 22.5 cm) end off.

Left Front

Chain 30 (33, 36). Work same as Back to armhole. Shape arm side same as Back, and, at the same time, decrease 1 stitch at neck edges, every other row, till there are 3 V stitches left. Work even, if necessary, to shoulder, end off.

Right Front

Work same as Left Front, reversing all armhole and neck shaping.

Finishing

Sew shoulder and side seams. Make picot edging as follows: starting at bottom right seam, work 1 row single crochet all around edges, making 3 single crochets in corners to turn, join with a slip stitch to first stitch. Next row, *chain 3, make 1 single crochet in the base of the chain 3, skip 1 stitch, make 1 single crochet in the next stitch, repeat from * all around. Make same edging around each armhole edge. Do not block.

young woman's
V-stitched
vest

young woman's loose-fitting tunic

Young Women's Sizes
Directions are for size 10. Changes for sizes 12 and 14 are in parentheses.

Materials
5 (5, 6) skeins (3.5 oz or 100 g each) Germantown Knitting Worsted by Brunswick or any knitting worsted to give gauge

Hooks
Size 10½ or K

Gauge
5 single crochets = 2 inches (5 cm)
To save time, take the time to check gauge.

Back
With size 10½ hook, chain 50 (52, 54) loosely to measure 18 (19, 20) inches (45, 47.5, 50 cm).

Foundation row: Work 1 single crochet in 2nd chain from hook, 1 single crochet in each chain thereafter [41 (51, 53) single crochets].

Row 1: Chain 2 to turn, skip the first 2 stitches, make 1 double crochet in the 3rd stitch, now make 1 double crochet in the 3rd stitch from hook, *skip 1 stitch, make 1 double crochet in the next stitch, now make 1 double crochet in the skipped stitch [cross-stitch made], repeat from * across row, ending with 1 double crochet in the top of the turning chain.

Row 2: Chain 1 to turn, make 1 single crochet in the 2nd stitch, 1 single crochet in each stitch across row, ending with 1 single crochet in the top of the turning chain.

Repeat Rows 1 and 2 till 14 (15, 16) inches (35, 37.5, 40 cm), or desired length to underarm. Place marker to show armhole, then continue in pattern as established till 6½ (7, 7½) inches (16.3, 17.5, 18.8 cm) above armhole marker, end off.

Front
Work same as Back till 4½ (5, 5½) inches (11.3, 12.5, 13.8 cm) above armhole marker. Shape neck as follows: Work pattern over 6 (6, 7) cross-stitches, chain 2, and turn. Working on this section only, decrease 1 stitch at neck edge, every row, till 4 cross-stitches are left. Work even, if necessary, to shoulder, end off.

Sleeves
Chain 48 (50, 52). Work pattern same as Back for 13 (14, 15) inches (32.5, 35, 37.5 cm), end off.

Collar
Chain 60 (64, 66). Work pattern same as Back for 6 inches (15 cm), end off.

Finishing
Sew shoulders, sew underarm seams up to underarm markers. Fold Sleeves in half and sew long ends together, then sew into armhole. Sew short ends of Collar together, then sew Collar in place. Work 1 row single crochet around all edges, end off. Do not block.

Young Woman's Loose-Fitting Tunic
*Easy to make and wear, this tunic will become a staple in any wardrobe. The basic
pattern is a cross-stitch, which is simply a variation of double crochet.*

four crocheted pillows

aran isle pillow

Size
12 inches (30 cm) square

Materials
2 skeins (1.8 or 50 g each) Shetland Look Yarn by Red Heart, or any yarn to give gauge
1 uncovered pillow form

Hook
Size 6 or G

Gauge
3 stitches = 1 inch (2.5 cm)
To save time, take the time to check gauge.

Patterns
Popcorn is worked on 1 stitch as follows: double crochet 5 times in same stitch, remove hook and insert in front of first double crochet in group, catch loop of last double crochet and draw through first double crochet, tighten stitch.

Post stitch is worked as follows: make double crochets from the back on wrong side rows and from the front on right side rows under the posts of the stitches in the row below.

Front
With size 6 hook, chain 39.
Foundation row: Make 1 double crochet in 3rd chain from hook, 1 double crochet in each stitch across row.
Row 1: Chain 3 to turn (double crochet under the post of the next-titch, 1 double crochet in each of next 2 stitches, double crochet under post of next stitch), double crochet in each of next 10 stitches, popcorn in next stitch, double crochet in next 10 stitches, repeat between ()'s ending 1 double crochet in top of turning chain.
Row 2: Chain 3 to turn, repeat between ()'s on Row 1, double crochet in each of the next 9 stitches, popcorn next stitch, double crochet in the next stitch, popcorn in next stitch, double crochet in next 9 stitches, repeat between ()'s of Row 1.
Row 3: Chain 3 to turn, repeat between ()'s of Row 1, double crochetnext 8 stitches, popcorn next stitch, double crochet next 3 stitches, popcorn next stitch, double crochet next 8 stitches, repeat between ()'s of Row 1.
Row 4: Chain 3 to turn, repeat between ()'s of Row 1, double crochet next 7 stitches, popcorn next stitch, double crochet next 5 stitches, popcorn next stitch, double crochet next 7 stitches, repeat between ()'s of Row 1.
Row 5: Chain 3 to turn, repeat between ()'s of Row 1, double crochet next 6 stitches, popcorn next stitch, double crochet next 3 stitches, popcorn next stitch, double crochet next 3 stitches, popcorn next stitch, double crochet next 6 stitches, repeat between ()'s of Row 1.
Row 6: Chain 3 to turn, repeat between ()'s of Row 1, double crochet next 5 stitches, popcorn next stitch, double crochet next 3 stitches,

Four Crocheted Pillows
Handmade pillows add a decorator touch to any room. They also make wonderful gifts, because they can be made quickly, easily, and inexpensively. Seen from left to right are: (first row) Aran Isle Pillow and Tweed Pillow, (second row) "Great Granny" Pillow and Lace-Look Pillow.

popcorn next stitch, double crochet next stitch, popcorn next stitch, double crochet next 3 stitches, popcorn next stitch, double crochet next 5 stitches, repeat between ()'s of Row 1.

Row 7: Chain 3 to turn, repeat between ()'s of Row 1, double crochet next 4 stitches, popcorn next stitch, double crochet next 3 stitches, popcorn next stitch, double crochet next 3 stitches, popcorn next stitch, double crochet next 3 stitches, popcorn next stitch, double crochet next 4 stitches, repeat between ()'s of Row 1.

Row 8: Chain 3 to turn, repeat between ()'s of Row 1, double crochet next 3 stitches, popcorn next stitch, double crochet next 3 stitches, popcorn next stitch, double crochet next 5 stitches, popcorn next stitch, double crochet next 3 stitches, popcorn next stitch, double crochet next 3 stitches, repeat between ()'s of Row 1.

Rows 9 through 15: Repeat Rows 7, 6, 5, 4, 3, 2, 1 in that order.

Row 16: Repeat between ()'s of Row 1, double crochet next 21 stitches, repeat between ()'s of Row 1, end off.

Back
Work same as Front.

Finishing

Hold pieces wrong side together. Working through both thicknesses, work 1 row single crochet around 3 sides, making 3 single crochets in each corner to turn. Slip pillow form inside cover, continue single crochet along 4th side of pillow, join with a slip stitch to first stitch, do not turn. Work 1 row backward single crochet all around.

tweed pillow

Size
14 inches (35 cm) square

Materials
2 skeins (1.8 oz or 50 g each) Red Heart Tweedy by Coats & Clark, or any tweed yarn to give gauge
1 uncovered pillow form

Hook
Size 10 or J

Gauge
3 stitches = 1 inch (2.5 cm)
To save time, take the time to check gauge.

Back
With size 10 hook, chain 39.
Foundation row: Work 1 single crochet, chain 2, 1 single crochet all in 3rd chain from hook, *skip 2 chains, work 1 single crochet, chain 2, 1 single crochet all in the next stitch, repeat from *, ending with 1 single crochet in the last stitch.
Row 1: Chain 2 to turn, *work 1 single crochet, chain 2, 1 single crochet in the chain-2 space from row below, repeat from * across row, end with 1 single crochet in the top of the turning chain.
   Repeat Row 1 for 14 inches (35 cm), end off.

Front
Work same as Back.

Finishing
Hold Back and Front, wrong sides together. Work single crochet all around through both thicknesses, making 3 single crochets in each corner to turn. Before joining last side, slip pillow form in place, continue crochet all around.

"great granny" pillow

Size
15 inches (37.5 cm) square

Materials
3 skeins (3.5 oz or 100 g each) Germantown Knitting Worsted by

Brunswick or any yarn to give gauge—1 skein each in Colors A,B, and C
1 uncovered pillow form

Hook   **Gauge**
Wooden size 15   2 double crochets = 1 inch (2.5 cm)
                  To save time, take the time to check gauge.

Note: Yarn is used double strand throughout.

Back

With size 15 hook and Color A, chain 4, join with a slip stitch to form a circle.

Row 1: Chain 4, (yarn over pick up a long loop) 4 times, yarn over and off all but last loop, yarn over and off 2 loops [puff stitch made] *chain 1, make 1 puff in ring, repeat from * 6 times more [8 puff stitches in all], join with a slip stitch to top of chain 4, break Color A.

Row 2: With Color B, chain 4, make 1 puff stitch behind the spaceof chain 4 in row below, chain 1, skip 1 puff, *3 double crochets in next space, chain 1, skip 1 puff, make 1 puff, chain 3, make 1 puff all in next space, chain 1, skip 1 puff, repeat from * twice more, skip 1 puff, make 3 double crochets in next space, chain 1, skip 1 puff, make 1 puff in same space as first puff, chain 3, join with a slip stitch to starting chain 4.

Row 3: Chain 4, make 1 puff in space behind chain 4 of row below * (chain 1, make 1 double crochet in next space) 4 times, chain 1, make 1 puff, chain 3, 1 puff all in next space, repeat from * twice more, (chain 1, 1 double crochet in next space) 4 times, chain 1, make 1 puff all in the same space as the one you started in, chain 3 join with a slip stitch to top of starting chain 4.

Row 4: Work as Row 2 except repeat between ( )'s 5 times. End off Color B.

Row 5: Join Color A in any corner space, make 5 single crochets in corner space, *1 single crochet in each space to next corner, 5 single crochets in corner space, repeat from * 2 times, 1 single crochet in each of the next 6 spaces, join with a slip stitch to starting chain. Break Color A.

Row 6: Join Color C in the center stitch of any corner, make 3 single crochets in corner stitch, * 1 single crochet in each stitch to next corner stitch, 3 single crochets in corner stitch, repeat from * 2 times, 1 single crochet in each of next single crochets, end with a slip stitchto first stitch.

Row 7: Chain 3, make 3 double crochets in corner stitch, *1 double crochet in each stitch to corner, 3 double crochets in corner, re-peatfrom * twice, 1 double crochet in each double crochet to end, join with a slip stitch to top of starting chain.

Row 8: Work same as Row 7, end off.

Front

Work same as Back.

Finishing

Holding pieces wrong sides together, work 1 row single crochet on 3 sides, working through double thickness and making 3 single crochets in each corner to turn. Slip pillow form in place, finish single crochet on 4th side, end off.

lace-look pillow

Size
9 by 18 inches (22.5 by 45 cm)

Materials
1 skein (3.5 oz 100 g or each) Germantown Knitting Worsted by Brunswick, or any knitting worsted to give gauge
1 cotton duck pillow in color to match yarn

Hook
Size 8 or H

Gauge
3 stitches = 1 inch (2.5 cm)
To save time, take the time to check gauge.

Note: Pillow is worked sideways.

Back
With size 8 or H hook, chain 33.
Foundation row: Work 1 single crochet in 2nd chain from hook, 1 single crochet in each chain thereafter.
Row 1: Chain 3 to turn, chain 2, skip 2, 1 double crochet in next stitch, *chain 2, skip 2, 1 double crochet in next stitch, repeat from * across ending 1 double crochet in last stitch.
Row 2: Chain 5, turn, *skip 2 chains, work 1 double crochet in next double crochet, chain 2, repeat from * ending 1 double crochet in the 3rd stitch of starting chain.
Row 3: Chain 3, turn, *2 double crochets in the chain-2 space, chain 1, repeat from * across ending 1 double crochet in the 3rd stitch of turning chain.
Row 4: Chain 5, turn, *skip 2 double crochets, make 1 double crochet in the chain-1 space, chain 3, (yarn over pick up a long loop) 3 times over the bar of the double crochet just made, yarn over and off all but last loop on hook, yarn over and off 2 [1 puff made], repeat from * across row, ending 1 double crochet in the 3rd stitch of starting chain 5. Repeat these 4 rows for 18 inches (45 cm), end off.

Front
Work same as Back.

Finishing
Hold both pieces, wrong sides together. Work 1 row single crochet through both thicknesses, on 3 sides of pillow. Put the pillow form in place, continue single crochet on 4th side, end off. Make 4 tassels for corners. [*To make tassels*: wind yarn 75 times around a 4-inch (10-cm) piece of cardboard. Tie one end, cut the other end. Tie a piece of yarn, round and round about 1 inch from top tie. Trim.]

64

Materials

11 skeins (3.5 oz or 100 g each) Red Heart 4-ply Knitting Worsted by Coats & Clark—10 in Color A and 1 in Color B—or any knitting worsted to give gauge

Hook	**Gauge**
Wooden size 15	1 cluster = 1 inch
	To save time, take the time to check gauge.

Note: Yarn is used double strand throughout.

Body

With size 15 hook and Color A, chain 100 stitches loosely.
Foundation row: Skip 2 chains, * 1 single crochet, 1 half double crochet, all in the next chain, skip 1 chain, repeat from * across row, end with 1 half double crochet in last stitch.
Row 1: Chain 2 to turn, *skip the half double crochet, make 1 single crochet, and 1 half double crochet all in the next single crochet, repeat from * across row, end with 1 half double crochet in last stitch.
   Repeat Row 1 till length is 40 inches (102.5 cm), end off.

Border

Foundation row: Join Color A in any corner space, * 1 single crochet to next corner space, 3 single crochets in corner space, repeat from * all around afghan (be sure to pick up same amount of stitches on corresponding sides), end with a slip stitch to starting chain.
Row 1: Chain 3, make 1 puff stitch in the next stitch, * chain 1, skip 1, 1 puff stitch in the next stitch, continue to make 1 puff stitch, chain 1, skip 1, till corner, in corner stitch make 1 puff stitch, chain 3, 1 puff stitch, repeat from * around, ending with a slip stitch to top of chain 3. [*To make a puff stitch:* yarn over hook and pull up a long loop, 3 times, yarn over and pull through all but the last loop, yarn over and pull through remaining loops.]
Row 2: Work same as Row 1.
Row 3: With Color B, repeat Foundation row.
Row 4: With Color A, repeat Foundation row.
End off. Do not block.

puff-bordered afghan

Puff-Bordered Afghan
Cuddle up in this warm afghan and let the winter winds blow. It is made in a simple pattern stitch on a large crochet hook and the yarn is used double strand.

Girl's Double-Breasted Suit
This smart little suit is a sure winner. It is easy to do in single crochet with a large hook and the yarn used double strand. Both the skirt and jacket can be worn with other outfits to stretch a girl's wardrobe.

jacket

girl's double-breasted suit

Girls' Sizes

Directions are for size 8. Changes for sizes 10 and 12 are in parentheses.

Materials

9 (10, 11) skeins (1.8 or 50 g each) Shetland Look Yarn by Red Heart, or any Shetland-type yarn to give gauge—8 skeins in Color A, 1 skein in Color B
6 button forms

Hooks
Size 6 or G
Size 10½ or K

Gauge
2 single crochets = 1 inch (2.5 cm)
To save time, take the time to check the gauge.

Note: Yarn is used double strand throughout except for buttons.

Back

With larger hook, chain 29 (31, 33).
Foundation row: Work 1 single crochet in 2nd chain from hook and 1 single crochet in each chain thereafter [28 (30, 32) single crochets].
Row 1: Chain 1 to turn, skip the first stitch [chain 1 counts as the first stitch], make 1 single crochet in each stitch to end of row.

Repeat Row 1 till back measures 7 (8, 9) inches (18, 21, 23 cm), or desired length to underarm. Slip stitch over the first 2 stitches, work single crochet to within 2 stitches of end of row. Do not work the last 2 stitches, chain 1, and turn. Continuing in pattern as established, decrease 1 stitch, each side, every other row, 3 times. Work even till armhole measures 6 (6½, 7) inches (15.5, 17, 18.5 cm), end off.

Left Front

Chain 21 (22, 23). Work same as Back to armhole, end at arm side. Slip stitch over 2 stitches, work to end of row. Chain 1, turn. Continuing in single crochet, decrease 1 stitch at arm edge, every other row, 3 times. Work even till armhole is 4½ (5, 6) inches (11.5, 13, 15.5 cm), ending at arm side. Chain 1, turn. Decrease 1 stitch at neck edge, every row, till there are 5 (6, 6) stitches left. Work even, if necessary, to shoulder, end off.

Right Front

Chain 20 (21, 22). Work same as Back to armhole, ending at front edge, chain 1, turn. Work single crochet to within 2 stitches of end of row, do not work last 2 stitches, chain 1, turn. Next row, decrease 1 stitch and repeat this decrease at arm side, every other row, 2 times more. Work even till armhole is 4½ (5, 6) inches (11.5, 13, 15.5 cm), ending at neck edge. Slip stitch over first 4 (5, 6) stitches. Work remaining 11 stitches. Continue in single crochet, decreasing 1 stitch neck edge, every row, till there are 5 (6, 6) stitches left. Work even to shoulder, end off.

67

Sleeves
Chain 21 (22, 23). Work in single crochet as for Back, till 10 (11, 12) inches (26, 28.5, 31 cm), or desired length to underarm. Slip stitch over 2 stitches, work to within 2 stitches of other side, chain 1, turn. Continue in single crochet, decreasing 1 stitch each side, every other row, 5 (6, 6) times. Work 1 (2, 2) row(s), end off.

Collar
Chain 21 (23, 25). Work in single crochet for 3 (3½, 4) inches (8, 9, 10 cm), end off.

Fronts and Collar Trim
With Color B and larger hook, starting at bottom right corner, and with right side facing you, work 1 row single crochet along front edge, end off. With Color A, starting in same place, work 1 row single crochet over the Color B row, end off. Starting at top, work Left Front to correspond. Trim is worked on 3 sides of collar, but not on the side to be sewn to jacket. With Color B, starting at bottom right corner, work single crochet along short edge, make 3 single crochets in corner, continue along top, make 3 single crochets in corner, work along other side, end off. With Color A, starting in same place, work 1 row single crochet over the Color B row, end off.

Buttons   *(make 6)*
With smaller hook and the yarn single strand, chain 4. Join with a slip stitch to form a ring, make 8 single crochets in center of ring. Make 2 single crochets in each stitch around. End off, leaving a long end for sewing. Place the button form in center of circle just made, gather edges up all around by sewing. Use same yarn to sew to Jacket as pictured. Single crochet is loosely done and buttons will fit easily into spaces, so that buttonholes are not necessary.

Finishing
Sew shoulder seams. Sew Collar in place. Center Collar with center back of jacket, having Collar reach around to beginning of neck shaping. Sew Sleeves in place, sew underarm seams. Block by soaking in cool water. Lay flat to dry. Do not steam.

Girls' Sizes
Directions are for size 8. Changes for sizes 10 and 12 are in parentheses.

skirt

Materials
3 (3, 4) skeins (1.8 oz or 50 g each) Shetland Look Yarn by Red Heart in Color A (for Color B use left-over yarn from jacket)

Hook
Size 10½

Gauge
2 single crochets = 1 inch (2.5 cm)
To save time, take the time to check gauge.

Note: Yarn is used single strand throughout.

Front
Chain 41 (43, 45). Work in single crochet as for Back of Jacket till 12 (13, 14) inches (31, 33, 36 cm), or 1 inch (2.5 cm) less than desired length. Next row, *1 single crochet in each of the next 2 stitches, pick up a loop in next 2 stitches, yarn over and through all loops on hook [decrease made]. Repeat from * across row, work 1 row, end off.

Back
Work same as for Front. Sew side seams.

Waistband
Starting at seam, join yarn, chain 5, * skip 1 single crochet, make 1 double crochet in next single crochet; chain 1, repeat from * all around, join with a slip stitch to 4th chain of starting chain. Chain 1, work 2 single crochets in each open space around, join with a slip stitch to starting chain, end off.

Suspenders *(make 2)*
Chain 60. Work 2 rows single crochet, end off. For front piece of Suspenders, chain 16, work 2 rows of single crochet, end off. Sew front piece to Suspenders about 5 inches from waist. With Color B, embroider little cross-stitches. With double strand of Color B, chain 100 (120, 120) for tie. Draw tie in and out of open spaces at waistband.

Finishing
Block by soaking in cool water, lay flat to dry. Do not steam.

boy's rugged pullover

Boy's Rugged Pullover
This beautifully textured pullover is sure to be a hit with the young set. Great for school or play, its classic good looks will go anywhere. The stitch is simple, the yarn is used double strand, and the crochet hook is large.

Boys' Sizes
Directions are for size 8. Changes for sizes 10 and 12 are in parentheses.

Materials
4 (5, 6) skeins (3.5 oz or 100 g each) Germantown Knitting Worsted by Brunswick, or any knitting worsted to give gauge

Hook
Size 10½ or K
Boye aluminum size N

Gauge
2 stitches = 1 inch (2.5 cm)
To save time, take the time to check gauge.

Note: Yarn is used double strand throughout.

Back

With smaller hook, chain 8 (8, 9).
Foundation row: Work 1 single crochet from the back loop in 2nd chain from hook, and 1 single crochet from the back loop in each chain to end of row [7 (7, 8) single crochets].
Row 1: Chain 1, turn, skip the first stitch [chain 1 counts as the first stitch], make 1 single crochet from the back loop in each stitch to end of row.

Repeat Row 1 for 26 (28, 30) rows. Do not break yarn. Working along long end of band just worked and using larger hook, pick up 1 single crochet in each row [26 (28, 30) single crochets]. Work in pattern stitch till 10½ (11, 11½) inches (25.3, 27.5, 28.8 cm) from the beginning. Slip stitch over 2 stitches, work to within 2 stitches of other side (do not work last 2 stitches). Decrease 1 stitch each side, every other row, 2 times. Work even till armhole is 6½ (6½, 7) inches (16.3, 16.3, 17.5 cm), end off.

Front

Work same as Back till armhole. Slip stitch over 2 stitches, work across next 10 (11, 12) stitches, chain 1, and turn. Working on this section only (this is Right Front), decrease 1 stitch arm side, every other row, twice, and, at the same time, decrease 1 stitch at neck edge, every 4th row, 2 (2, 3) times [4 (5, 5) stitches left]. Work even till armhole is 6½ (6½, 7) inches (16.3, 16.3, 17.5 cm), end off. Skip 2 center stitches, join yarn, work other Left Front to correspond.

Sleeves

With smaller hook, chain 8 (8, 9). Work Foundation row and Row 1 same as Back. Repeat Row 1 for 16 (18, 20) rows. Do not break yarn. Using larger hook and working along the long end of band, pick up 16 (18, 20) single crochets. Work in pattern stitch till 12 (13, 14) inches (30, 32.5, 35 cm), or desired length to underarm. Slip stitch over 2 stitches, work to within 2 stitches of other side, then decrease 1 stitch each side, every other row, 3 times. Work even till cap of Sleeve is 5½ (5½, 6) inches (13.8, 13.8, 15 cm), end off.

Collar

With smaller hook, chain 5, work single crochet from the back loop for 6 rows, then increase 1 stitch on 1 side only, every row, 6 times. Work even in pattern as established till 36 (38, 38) rows in all, then decrease 1 stitch same side, every row, 6 times. Work 6 rows even, end off.

Finishing

Sew shoulders and underarm seams. Set in sleeves. Pin Collar in place, centering back, and overlapping Fronts from left to right, sew in place. Do not block.

man's nubby tweed cardigan

Men's Sizes
Directions are for size 38. Changes for sizes 40 and 42 are in parentheses.

Materials
7 (7, 8) skeins (3.5 oz or 100 g each) Super Heavy Donegal Tweed by Tahki or any tweed yarn to give gauge
7 (7, 8) skeins (3.5 oz or 100 g each) Donegal Homespun by Tahki, or any tweed yarn to give gauge

Hook
Plastic size Q

Gauge
1½ stitches = 1 inch (2.5 cm)

Note: Yarn is used 1 strand of each held together throughout.

Back
With size Q hook, chain 22 (24, 26).
Foundation row: Work 1 double crochet in 2nd chain from hook *1 single crochet in next stitch, 1 double crochet in next stitch, repeat from * across row.
Row 1: Chain 1 to turn [chain 1 counts as the first single crochet], skip the first double crochet, *make 1 double crochet over the next single crochet, make 1 single crochet over the next double crochet, repeat from * across row, ending with 1 double crochet over the turning chain.

Repeat Row 1 till 16 (16, 16½) inches (40, 40, 41.3 cm), or desired length to underarm. Slip stitch over 1 stitch, work to within 1 stitch of other side, chain 1, and turn. Decrease 1 stitch each side once only, then, continuing in pattern, work even till armhole is 9 (9½, 10) inches (22.5, 23.8, 25 cm), end off.

Left Front
Chain 11 (12, 13). Work pattern same as Back to armhole. Shape arm side same as Back, and, at the same time, decrease 1 stitch neck edge, every other row, till 5 (6, 6) stitches remain. Work even till shoulder, end off.

Sleeves
Chain 12 (13, 14). Work same pattern as Back, increasing 1 stitch each side, every 3 inches (7.5 cm), 5 (6, 6) times. Work even till 18 (18½, 18½) inches (45, 45.3, 45.3 cm), or desired length to underarm. Slip stitch over 1 stitch, work to within 1 stitch of other side, chain, and turn. Continuing in pattern, decrease 1 stitch each side, every other row, for 6½ (7, 7½) inches (16.3, 17.5, 18.8 cm), end off.

Finishing
Sew all seams. Starting at bottom of Right Front, work 3 rows of single crochet all around front and neck edges, making 5 buttonholes on Left Front on second row of crochet. [*To make buttonholes:* chain 1, skip 1 stitch. On 3rd row, make 1 single crochet in the buttonhole space.]

Man's Nubby Tweed Cardigan
*Take two great yarns, a large hook, and some easy stitches and you have all the
ingredients for this terrific cardigan. It is an easy project for beginners, but seasoned
crocheters will love it too.*

Man's Hat and Scarf Set
When the temperatures drop and the snowflakes fall, this cozy hat and scarf set will chase the chills away.

Sizes
One size fits all.

Materials
3 skeins (3.5 oz or 100 g each) Germantown Knitting Worsted by
Brunswick, or any knitting worsted to give gauge

Hooks
Size 10½ or K
Boye aluminum size N

Gauge
2 single crochets = 1 inch (2.5 cm)
To save time, take the time to check gauge.

Note: Yarn is used double strand throughout.

man's hat and scarf set

hat

Body
With larger hook, chain 36.
Foundation row: Work 1 single crochet in 2nd chain from hook, 1
single crochet in each stitch across row [35 single crochets].
Row 1: Chain 1 to turn, skip the first stitch [chain 1 counts as the
first stitch], 1 single crochet in each stitch across row.
   Repeat Row 1 till 4½ inches (11.3 cm). Next row, work as follows:
*Pick up a loop in each of the next 2 stitches, yarn over hook and
through all loops on hook [decrease made], 1 single crochet in each
of next 2 stitches, repeat from * across row. Repeat the last row, 2
times more, end off, leaving a long end for sewing. Thread this long
end on a yarn needle, gather top of hat and sew back seam.

Border
With smaller hook, chain 9, work single crochet from the back loop
for 21 inches (52.5 cm), end off.

Finishing
Sew short ends of Border, sew Border to bottom of Hat. Do not block.

scarf

With larger hook, chain 100. Work in single crochet same as Hat
for 8 inches (20 cm), end off.

toddler's drawstring pullover

Toddlers' Sizes
Directions are for size 2. Changes for sizes 3 and 4 are in parentheses.

Materials
6 (7, 8) skeins (2 oz or 56 g each) Nubs and Slubs by Stanley Berocco, or any nubby yarn to give gauge

Hook
Size 10½ or K

Gauge
2 stitches = 1 inch (2.5 cm)
To save time, take the time to check gauge.

Note: Yarn is used double strand throughout.

Back and Sleeves

With size 10½ hook, chain 29 (31, 33).
Foundation row: Work 1 single crochet in 2nd chain from hook, 1 single crochet in each chain thereafter [28 (30, 32) single crochets].
Row 1: Chain 2 and turn, skip the first stitch [chain 2 counts as the first double crochet], make 1 double crochet in each stitch to end of row.
Row 2: Chain 1 to turn, skip the first stitch [chain 1 counts as the first single crochet], make 1 single crochet in each stitch to end of row, 1 single crochet in top of turning chain.

Repeat Rows 1 and 2 till 8 (9, 10) inches (20, 22.5, 25 cm), or desired length to underarm, ending on a double crochet row. On the next row, chain 14 (15, 16). Turn and work single crochet on the added chain, continue single crochet along Back, then, at end of row, chain 16 (17, 18). Next row, make 1 double crochet in 3rd chain from hook, 1 double crochet in each remaining chain. Continue double crochet across Back and other Sleeve. Continue working in pattern as established across all stitches till piece measures 4 (4½, 5) inches (10, 11.3, 12.5 cm) from added-on chains. End off.

Front

Work same as Back till piece measures 1 (1½, 2) inches (2.5, 3.8, 5 cm) above added-on chain. Then work neckline shaping as follows: work across 21 (22, 23) stitches, chain, and turn. Work on this side only in pattern till same length as back to shoulder, end off. Skip the center stitches, join yarn 21 (22, 23) stitches in from other side and work to correspond.

Finishing

Sew shoulder seams, sew underarm seams, leaving 3 (3½, 3½) inches (7.5, 8.8, 8.8 cm) at bottom open for slits. Make 2 chains of 55 (60, 65) stitches each for drawstrings. Run drawstrings in and out of stitches at bottom. Do not block.

Toddler's Drawstring Pullover
*Anyone who has ever dressed a toddler knows that getting him into a pullover is not
easy. The wide neck and drawstring on this one make it easy to get on and off.*

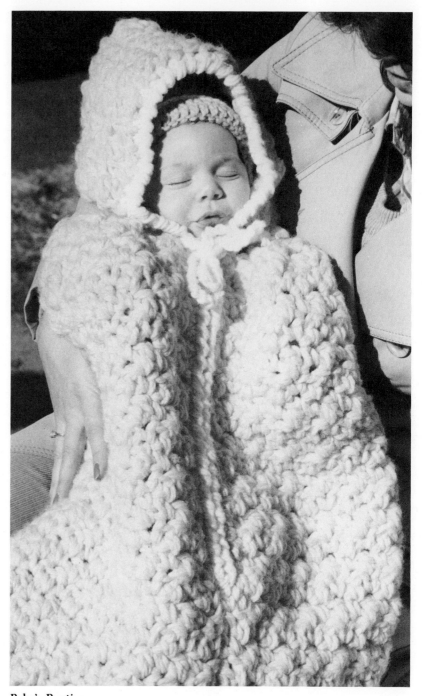

Baby's Bunting
The long zipper and loose-fitting hood make this bunting ideal for keeping baby warm in cold weather.

Infants' Size
One size fits all.

Materials
9 skeins (4 oz or 112 g each) Big Berella Bulky by Bernat, or any bulky yarn to give gauge

Hook
Wooden size 15

Gauge
1½ stitches = 1 inch (2.5 cm)

Note: Yarn is used double strand throughout.
Bunting is 1 piece up to neck; the hood is picked up.

baby's bunting

Bunting
With size 15 hook, chain 62.
Foundation row: Work 1 single crochet in 2nd chain from hook, *1 double crochet in next stitch, 1 single crochet in the next stitch, repeat from * across row.
Row 1: Chain 2, turn, skip the first single crochet [chain 2 counts as a double crochet], make 1 single crochet in the next double crochet, *1 double crochet in the next single crochet, 1 single crochet in the next double crochet, repeat from * across ending with 1 single crochet in the top of the turning chain.

Repeat Row 1 till bunting measures 22 inches (55 cm). On the next row, *pick up a loop in each of the next 2 stitches, yarn over and off all loops on hook, repeat from * across row. Chain 3, turn. Next row, skip 1 stitch, *1 double crochet in next stitch, chain 1, skip 1, repeat from * across row. Next row, work 30 single crochets across top of open-work row.

Hood
Now work pattern same as body of Bunting on these 30 stitches for 9 inches (22.5 cm), end off.

Finishing
Sew top of Hood. Fold bunting so that ends meet in front, sew bottom seam. Sew front seam up 6 inches (15 cm) from bottom. Starting at bottom of front opening, on right side, work 1 row single crochet up front, all around Hood, and down other side. Do not turn, do not break yarn. Work 1 row single crochet backwards around stitches just worked, end off. Using doubled yarn, chain 100. Weave chain in and out open row at neckline. Do not block.

girl's striped-yoked pullover

Young Women's Sizes

Directions are for size 10. Changes for sizes 12 and 14 are in parentheses.

Materials

7 (8, 8) skeins (3.5 oz or 100 g each) Red Heart 4-ply Knitting Worsted by Coats & Clark or any knitting worsted to give gauge—5 (6, 6) skeins in Color A, 1 skein each in Colors B and C

Hook

Boye aluminum size N

Gauge

2 stitches = 1 inch (2.5 cm)
To save time, take the time to check gauge.

Note: Yarn is worked double strand throughout.

Pieces are made up to armhole, then Yoke is worked round and round as 1 piece.

Back

With size N hook and Color A, chain 32 (34, 36).
Foundation row: Work 1 single crochet in 2nd chain from hook and 1 single crochet in each stitch across row [31 (33, 35) single crochets].
Row 1: Chain 2 to turn, skip the first stitch [chain 2 counts as first stitch], make 1 double crochet in each stitch across [do not break Color A].
Row 2: Join Color B, chain 1, skip the first stitch, work 1 single crochet in each stitch across row.
Row 3: Chain 1, turn, work 1 row single crochet.
Row 4: With Color A, chain 2, skip the first stitch, work 1 double crochet in each stitch across row.
Row 5: Chain 1, turn, skip the first stitch, work 1 single crochet in each stitch across row.
Row 6: Join Color C, work 1 row single crochet.
Row 7: Chain 1, turn, skip the first stitch, work 1 single crochet in each stitch across row.
Row 8: With Color A, chain 2, skip the first stitch, work 1 double crochet in each stitch across row.
Row 9: Chain 1, turn, skip the first stitch, work 1 row single crochet.
Row 10: Join Color B, chain 1, skip the first stitch, work 1 single crochet in each stitch across row.
Row 11: Chain 1, turn, skip the first stitch, work 1 single crochet in each stitch across row.
Row 12: With Color A, chain 2, skip the first stitch, work 1 double crochet in each stitch across row.
Row 13: Chain 1, turn, skip the first stitch, work 1 single crochet in each stitch across row.

Repeat Rows 12 and 13 till 12 (12½, 13) inches (30, 31.3, 32.5 cm) from beginning, end on a double crochet row. End off and set this section aside.

Girl's Striped-Yoked Pullover

Stripes are an easy way to add contrast and color to classic shapes. The stripes on the yoke make this pullover colorful and cheerful to wear.

Front

Work same as Back.

Sleeves

Chain 22 (24, 26). Work pattern same as Back, end off. Make another Sleeve the same, do not break yarn.

Yoke

With same yarn that is attached to Sleeve, work single crochet along top of Back. Continue to work along top of first Sleeve, then continue along top of Front and remaining Sleeve. Join with a slip stitch to first stitch of Back. Mark the end of this Sleeve for Back joining. All pieces should now be joined in a circle. Yoke will be worked in 1 piece, round and round.

Row 1: Chain 2, work 1 double crochet in each of next 5 stitches, yarn over, draw up a loop in next stitch, yarn over, and draw up a loop in the next stitch, yarn over, draw through all 3 loops on hook [decrease made]. *Work 1 double crochet in each of next 6 stitches, decrease over next 2 stitches, repeat from * around, end by joining with a slip stitch top of starting chain 2.

Row 2: Join Color B, chain 1, work 1 row single crochet, end with a slip stitch to top of starting chain.

Row 3: Repeat Row 1, except have 4 stitches between each decrease.

Row 4: Join Color C, chain 1, work single crochet, decreasing after every 3rd stitch.

Row 5: With Color A, work in double crochet, decreasing after every 2nd stitch.

Row 6: With Color A, work single crochet, decreasing every other stitch.

Row 7: With Color A, work 1 row double crochet.

Rows 8 and 9: With Color A, work 1 row single crochet.

Row 10: With Color A, work 1 row backward single crochet.

Finishing

Sew all underarm seams. With yarn double strand, chain 80, for tie. Weave in and out at neck. Work 1 row single crochet and 1 row backward single crochet around bottom of Sleeves. Do not block.

baby's snowsuit

The interesting texture of this snowsuit is achieved by combining single crochet and double crochet. This method creates a closely woven stitch that is sure to keep baby warm and cozy.

Infants' Sizes
Directions are for size 9 months. Changes for sizes 18 months and 2 years are in parentheses.

Materials
5 (5, 5) skeins (3.5 oz or 100 g each) Red Heart 4-ply Knitting Worsted by Coats & Clark, or any knitting worsted to give gauge —4 skeins in Color A, 1 skein in Color B
5 buttons for Jacket
2 buttons for Leggings

Hook
Size 10½ or K

Gauge
3 stitches = 1 inch (2.5 cm)
To save time, take the time to check gauge.

83

jacket

Back

With size 10½ hook and Color A, chain 32 (34, 36).

Foundation row: Work 1 double crochet in 2nd chain from hook, *1 single crochet in the next stitch, 1 double crochet in the next stitch, repeat from * across row.

Row 1: Chain 1 to turn [skip the first double crochet, chain 1 counts as the first single crochet], make 1 double crochet in the next single crochet, *make 1 single crochet in the next double crochet, make 1 double crochet in the next single crochet, repeat from * across row.

Repeat Row 1 till 7½ (8, 8½) inches (18.8, 20, 21.3 cm) from the beginning. Slip stitch across 2 stitches, work to within 2 stitches of other side, chain, and turn. Continuing in pattern, decrease 1 stitch each side, every row, 2 times. Work even till armhole is 4½ (5, 5½) inches (11.3, 12.5, 13.8 cm), end off.

Left Front

Chain 14 (15, 16). Work same as Back to armhole. At the arm side, slip stitch over 2 stitches, work across row. Continuing in pattern, decrease 1 stitch arm side only, every row, 2 times. Work even till armhole is 2½ (3, 3½) inches (6, 7.5, 9 cm), ending at front edge. Slip stitch over 3 stitches, then decrease 1 stitch front edge, every row, 2 times. Work even to shoulder, end off.

Right Front

Work same as Left Front, reversing all shaping.

Sleeves

Chain 24 (24, 26). Work in pattern same as Back, increasing 1 stitch each side, every 2 inches (5 cm), 3 (3, 4) times. Work even till Sleeve is 7½ (8, 8½) inches (18.8, 20, 21.3 cm). Slip stitch over 2 stitches, work to within 2 stitches of other side, chain, and turn. Continuing in pattern, decrease 1 stitch each side, every row, 5 (6, 7) times. Work 1 (1, 2) row(s) even. On the next row, work 2 stitches together all across row, end off.

Collar

Chain 31 (33, 35). Work pattern same as Back for 1 row. Do not break yarn, join Color B, work 2 rows, break Color B. Continue with Color A till Collar is 2½ (2½, 3) inches (6, 6, 7.5 cm), end off.

Finishing

Sew shoulder seams. Sew underarm seams and set in Sleeves. Joining Color A on bottom Right Front, work 2 rows single crochet along front edge, do not break Color A, join Color B, work 2 rows. Buttonholes are to be made on the 2nd row of Color B, right side for girls, left side for boys. (*To make buttonholes:* Chain 2, skip 1. On next row, make 1 single crochet in the chain-2 space.) Break Color B, work 2 more rows Color A, end off. Starting at top Left Front, work border to correspond. Sew Collar in place, centering in back, and having Collar end at buttonhole row. Work 1 row single crochet around Collar, making 3 single crochets in each corner to turn. Work 1 row Color A, 1 row Color B around Sleeves.

84

Chain 42 (44, 46). Work Color B same as Back for 2 rows, do not break Color B, join Color A, and work 2 rows. Repeat the last 4 rows once more. Break Color B. Continuing in Color A, work in pattern till 6 (6½, 7) inches (15, 16.3, 17.5 cm) from the beginning. Continuing in single crochet, on the next row, decrease every 3rd stitch. On the next row, decrease every other stitch. Work 1 row even, end off, leaving a long end for sewing. With this long end, gather top, sew back seam. Fold back cuff 6 rows.

Earlaps

Starting 1 inch over from back seam, pick up 10 stitches, work pattern for 2 rows. Then, continuing in pattern, decrease 1 stitch each side, every row, till 2 stitches remain, end off.

Finishing

Starting at top side of one Earlap, work single crochet to bottom of Earlap, chain 30, work single crochet along chain, then continue single crochet along other side of earlap. Work other side to correspond. Do not block.

Left Side   *(Back and Front)*

Chain 38 (42, 46). Work pattern same as Back till 10 (10½, 11) inches (22.5, 23.8, 24) to crotch. Slip stitch over 2 stitches, work to within 2 stitches of the side, chain and turn. Decrease 1 stitch each side, every row, 2 times. Work even till 4 (4½, 5) inches (10, 11.3, 12.5 cm) from crotch. Slip stitch over 4 stitches. Work pattern on next 7 (9, 11) stitches. Chain and turn [this is front bib section]. Continue on these 7 (9, 11) stitches for 4 (4½, 5) inches (10, 11.3, 12.5 cm), end off. Skip 6 stitches in center, work 11 (13, 15) remaining stitches. Work on these stitches for 3½ inches (9 cm), ending at back side edge. Slip stitch over 4 stitches, working on remaining 7 (9, 11) stitches till piece is 5 (5½, 6) inches (12.5, 13.8, 15 cm) from last group of 4 slip stitches. Now decrease 1 stitch each side, every row, till 1 stitch remains, end off.

Right Side   *(Back and Front)*

Work to correspond to Left Side, reversing all shaping.

Finishing

Fold each piece in half and sew leg up to crotch. Sew back of Left and Right Sides together from crotch to top. Sew front of Left and Right Sides together from crotch to top. Starting at underarm, work 1 row single crochet and 1 row backward single crochet around entire top edge of Leggings. Sew a button at top of each front section. Button will button anywhere on strap, as needed. Do not block.

girl's fluffy vest

Girls' Sizes
Directions are for size 10. Changes for sizes 12 and 14 are in parentheses.

Materials
3 (4, 4) skein (1.7 or 50 g each) Fluffy Yarn by Unger, or any brushed yarn to give gauge
2 skeins (3.5 oz or 100 g each) Germantown Knitting Worsted by Brunswick in a contrasting color

Hooks
Wooden size 15

Gauge
1½ stitches = 1 inch (2.5 cm)
To save time, take the time to check gauge.

Note: Yarn is used double strand throughout.
    Stitches must be worked very loosely.

Back
With size 15 hook and knitting worsted, chain 25 (27, 29).
Foundation row: Work 1 single crochet in 2nd chain from hook, 1 single crochet in each chain to end of row [24 (26, 28) single crochets]. The piece should measure 16 (17, 18) inches (40, 42.5, 45 cm).
Row 1: Chain 1 to turn, skip the first stitch [chain 1 counts as the first stitch], make 1 single crochet in each stitch to end of row. Do not break knitting worsted.
Row 2: Chain 3 with Fluffy yarn [chain 3 counts as first double crochet], *chain 1, skip 1, make 1 double crochet in each of next 2 stitches, repeat from * across row, ending with chain 1 skip 1, 1 double crochet in top of the turning chain.
Row 3: Chain 1 to turn. Repeat Row 1. Do not break Fluffy yarn.
Row 4: Chain 1 with knitting worsted (chain 1 counts as first single crochet). *Make 1 long half double crochet in the skipped stitch two rows below, make 1 single crochet in each of the next 2 stitches, repeat from * across row, ending 1 long half double crochet in skipped stitch, 1 single crochet in the top of the turning chain. [*To make a long half double crochet:* yarn over and pull up a long loop, yarn over and off all 3 loops on hook.]
    Repeat Rows 1–4 for pattern, carrying yarn up each time. Work till 14 (15, 16) inches (35, 37.5, 40 cm), or desired length to underarm, ending with Row 4. Slip stitch over 4 stitches, work to within 4 stitches of other side, chain 3 with Fluffy yarn, and continue in pattern till armhole is 7 (7½, 8) inches (17.5, 18.8, 20 cm), end off.

Front
Work same as Back till armhole is 1 inch (2.5 cm), ending with Row 4. Work to center, chain, and turn. Work on this section only for 3 inches (7.5 cm), ending at neck edge. Slip stitch over 6 stitches, work remaining stitches till piece measures same as Back to shoulder, end off. Join yarn at center and work other side to correspond, reversing neck shaping.

Girl's Fluffy Vest
The unique use of color and stitches gives this vest an unusual look. It is easier to make than you would think, but it is not a project for beginners.

Finishing

Sew shoulder seams and underarm seams. With knitting worsted, work 2 rows of single crochet around all edges. Do not block.

Young Woman's Turtleneck Pullover

Turtleneck pullovers are very popular with the younger crowd. The yarn is crinkly soft, the stitch double crochet. If you wish, this sweater can easily be turned into a crew-neck pullover by making the neckline only 1 inch high.

Young Women's Sizes

Directions are for size 10. Changes for sizes 12 and 14 are in parentheses.

Materials

10 (10, 11) skeins (1.7 oz or 50 g each) Rhumba Yarn by Unger, or any knitting worsted to give gauge

Hook
Size 10½ or K

Gauge
2 stitches = 1 inch (2.5 cm)
To save time, take the time to check gauge.

Note: Yarn is used double strand throughout.

Back

With size 10½ hook, chain 32 (34, 36).
Foundation row: Make 1 double crochet in 3rd chain from hook, make 1 double crochet in each chain across row [30 (32, 34) double crochets].
Row 1: Chain 3 to turn, skip the first stitch [chain 3 counts as the first double crochet], make 1 double crochet in each stitch across row, make 1 double crochet in top of the turning chain.

Repeat Row 1 till 10 (11, 12) inches (25, 27.5, 30 cm), or desired length to underarm. Slip stitch over 3 stitches, work to within 3 stitches of other side, chain 3, and turn. Continuing in pattern as established, decrease 1 stitch each side, every row, 2 times. Work even on the remaining 20 (22, 24) stitches till armhole is 7 (7, 7½) inches (17.5, 17.5, 18.8 cm), end off.

Front

Work as Back till armhole is 5 (5, 5½) inches (12.5, 12.5, 13.8 cm). Work across 7 (7, 8) stitches, chain 2, and turn. Working on these stitches only, decrease 1 stitch neck edge, every row, 3 times. Work even till same as Back to shoulder, end off. Skip the center 6 (8, 8) stitches, join yarn, and work 7 (7, 8) stitches other side. Work to correspond, end off.

Sleeves

With size 10½ hook, chain 17 (18, 19). Work pattern same as Back, increasing 1 stitch each side, every 2 inches (5 cm), 5 (5, 6) times. Work even till 14 (15, 16) inches (35, 37.5, 40 cm), or desired length to underarm. Slip stitch over 3 stitches, work to within 3 stitches of other side, then decrease 1 stitch each side, every row, 5 (7, 7) times. Work 1 row even, end off.

Collar

Chain 34 (36, 38). Work pattern same as Back for 5 inches (12.5 cm), end off.

Finishing

Sew shoulder seams, seam short ends of Collar, and sew in place. Sew underarm seams. Work 1 row single crochet around Sleeve, Collar, and botton edges. Do not block.

young woman's turtleneck pullover

young woman's shell-stitched cardigan

Young Women's Sizes
Directions are for size 10. Changes for sizes 12 and 14 are in parentheses.

Materials
10 (12, 12) skeins (1.7 oz or 50 g each) Fluffy yarn by Unger, or any brushed yarn to give gauge

Hook
Size 10½ or K

Gauge
2 stitches = 1 inch (2.5 cm)
To save time, take the time to check gauge.

Note: Yarn is used double strand throughout.
   The stitch used is a long double crochet and must be worked very loosely.

Back and Fronts *(to armhole)*

With size 10½ hook, chain 67 (69, 71) stitches loosely.

Foundation row: 1 single crochet in 2nd chain from hook, 1 single crochet in each chain across row [66 (68, 70) single crochets].

Row 1: Chain 3 to turn, make a long half double crochet in the first single crochet, *skip next single crochet, single crochet in the next single crochet, skip 2 single crochets, work 3 long half double crochets in next single crochet [shell made]. [*To make a long half double crochet:* pull up a long loop to measure 1 inch, yarn over, and draw through all 3 loops on hook.] Repeat from * across row, ending with 1 single crochet, skip 2, 2 long half double crochets in the last stitch. [You should have 12 (13, 14) shells, with a half shell on each side].

Row 2: Chain 1, turn, 1 single crochet in first stitch, *shell in next single crochet, working through all 3 loops of the half double crochet, make a single crochet in the center stitch of the next shell, repeat from * across, ending with a shell in last single crochet, skip the next half double crochet, single crochet in the top of the turning chain.

Row 3: Chain 3 to turn, make a long half double crochet in first single crochet, *single crochet through all 3 loops of center stitch of next shell, shell in next single crochet, repeat from * across to last single crochet, make 2 long half double crochets in the last single crochet.

   Repeat Rows 2 and 3 till piece measures 10 (11, 12) inches (25, 27.5, 30 cm), or desired length to underarm, ending with Row 2 of pattern. Do not break yarn.

Right Front Top

On Row 3, work across half shell at beginning of row and 2 (2, 2½) shells plus the single crochet, chain, and turn. Continue in pattern as established till this section is 6½ (7, 7½) inches (16.3, 17.5, 18.8 cm) from the armhole, ending at front edge. Chain 2 and turn, work half shell, 1 shell, and the single crochet. Continue on these stitches only for 3½ (4, 4) inches (8.8, 10, 10 cm) more [this section becomes the collar], end off.

90

Young Woman's Shell-Stitched Cardigan
The combination of stitches and fluffy yarn give this jacket a unique look. Hard-to-please teenagers will just love it.

Left Front Top

Join yarn at single crochet 2 (2, 2½) shells in from other side and complete same as Right Front Top, reversing armhole and collar shaping.

Back Top

Skip 1 shell for underarm, work to within 1 shell of other Front, chain 2, and turn. Continue in pattern till Back is 6½ (7, 7½) inches (16.3, 17.5, 18.8 cm), end off.

Sleeves

Chain 16 (18, 18). Work pattern same as Back, increasing 1 double crochet each side, every 3 inches, 5 (5, 6) times. Work even till 15 (15½, 16) inches (37.5, 38.8, 40 cm), or desired length to underarm. Slip stitch over 2 double crochets, work to within 2 double crochets of other side, chain 2, and turn. Continue in pattern as established till cap is 7 (7½, 8) inches (17.5, 18.8, 20 cm). On next row, work in single crochet, working 2 stitches together all across row to gather top of sleeve.

Finishing

Sew shoulder, sew back of collar pieces together, sew collar in place. Sew underarm seams of Sleeve, set sleeve in. Crochet border as follows: Starting at bottom, join yarn where a side seam would be, work 3 rows of single crochet around all outside edges, making 3 single crochets in each corner and making 5 buttonholes on the 2nd row. [*To make buttonholes:* chain 2 and skip 1 stitch. On the 3rd row, make 1 single crochet in the buttonhole space.] At the end of the 3rd row, join with a slip to first stitch. Do not continue foreward, work 1 row of backward single crochet all around. Work same border around bottom of Sleeves. Do not block.

woman's oriental jacket

Woman's Oriental Jacket
Easy, a loose fit, Mandarin collar, side slits, and tiny buttons—all add up to a lovely Oriental look. This jacket completes any outfit.

Women's Sizes
Directions are for small size. Changes for medium and large sizes are in parentheses.

Materials
7 (8, 8) skeins (3.5 oz or 100 g each) Germantown Knitting Worsted by Brunswick, or any knitting worsted to give gauge
9 buttons

Hooks
Size 10½ or K
Boye aluminum size N

Gauge

1 pattern sequence = 1 inch (2.5 cm)

Note: Yarn is used double strand throughout.

Back

With size N hook, chain 37 (39, 40).

Foundation row: Starting in 2nd chain from hook, *make 1 single crochet, chain 1, 1 single crochet all in the same stitch, skip 1 stitch, repeat from * across row, ending with 1 single crochet in last chain.

Row 1: Chain 1 to turn, skip the first stitch, *1 single crochet, chain 1, 1 single crochet all in the next single crochet [this is the first single crochet in the cluster from row below], skip the chain 1, and the next single crochet, repeat from * across row, ending with 1 single crochet in the last stitch.

Continue to repeat Row 1 till 14½ (15, 16) inches (36.3, 37.5, 40 cm) from the beginning. Slip stitch over 2 (2, 3) stitches, work to within 2 (2, 3) stitches of other side, chain 1, and turn. Continue to keep pattern as established, decrease 1 stitch each side, every other row, 2 times. Work even till armhole is 7 (7½, 8) inches (17.5, 18.8, 20 cm), end off.

Left Front

Chain 20 (22, 24). Work same as Back to armhole. Shape arm side as Back. Keep front edges even, work till armhole is 5 (5½, 6) inches (12.5, 13.8, 15 cm). Shape neck as follows: At neck edge, slip stitch over 7 stitches, then decrease 1 stitch neck edge, every row, 2 (3, 3) times. Work even on remaining stitches to shoulder, end off.

Right Front

Work same as Left Front, reversing all arm side and neck shaping.

Sleeves

Chain 10 (12, 14). Work pattern same as Back for 9 rows. Break yarn and set this piece aside. Make another piece the same, do not break yarn. On the next row, work across, chain 1, then continue row across piece that was set aside. Continue in pattern as 1 piece, increasing 1 stitch, each side, every 5 inches (12.5 cm), 2 times. Work even till sleeve measures 15½ (16, 17) inches (38.8, 40, 41.3 cm) or ½ inch (1.25 cm) less than desired finished length. Slip stitch over 2 (2, 3) stitches, work to within 2 (2, 3) stitches of other side, chain 1, and turn. Continuing in pattern, decrease 1 stitch each side, every other row, 6 (7, 8) times, end off.

Collar

Chain 32 (35, 37). Work pattern same as Back for 1½ inches (3.8 cm), end off.

Pockets

Chain 16 (17, 18). Work pattern same as Back for 6 inches (15 cm), end off.

Finishing

Sew shoulders. Sew underarm seams, leaving 5 inches (12.5 cm) open from bottom for slits. Sew Sleeves and set in. Sew on Pockets, sew Collar in place, centering back and leaving 1 inch (2.5 cm) free from front edges. With right side facing you and starting at top of right side slit, work 1 row single crochet along slit, make 3 single crochets in corner to turn, continue single crochet along bottom edge, make 3 single crochets in corner to turn, continue along Right Front edge, making 7 buttonloops, starting about 14 inches (35 cm) from bottom [*To make buttonloops*: chain 4, skip 1 stitch.] Continue in single crochet all around in this manner, always making 3 single crochets in corners to turn. When you are back to where you started, join with a slip stitch to first single crochet. Do not turn. Working single crochet backwards, work another row all around jacket. Starting at top of slit on Sleeves, make same edging on Sleeves. Do not block.

index